Robert Calow

Agnes, the Bower of Souls

And Other Poems

Robert Calow

Agnes, the Bower of Souls
And Other Poems

ISBN/EAN: 9783337006525

Printed in Europe, USA, Canada, Australia, Japan

Cover: Foto ©Thomas Meinert / pixelio.de

More available books at **www.hansebooks.com**

AGNES,

THE BOWER OF SOULS,

AND OTHER POEMS.

BY

ROBERT CALOW.

LONDON AND SYDNEY:
REMINGTON AND CO., LIMITED,

MDCCCXCIII.

All Rights Reserved.

CONTENTS.

		PAGE
FANCY	.. ..	1
A ZEPHYR	.. ..	2
THE MERRY SONGSTERS..	.. ..	4
CUPID SCORNED	.. ..	5
THE HOLIDAY	.. ..	6
EARLY DAWN ..	.. ..	9
ANXIETY	.. ..	11
THE HONEYSUCKLE ..	.. ..	12
REST NOT ..	.. ..	14
A SACK OF FLOUR (HUMOROUS)	.. .. ..	18
TO MAIDENS	.. ..	25
ANTOINE'S SONG	.. ..	27
THE ORPHAN	.. ..	28
HOPE	.. ..	29
THE MARCH OF LIFE	.. ..	30
SPRING	.. ..	34
AUTUMN	.. ..	36
GOLD	.. ..	38
MY LOVE ..	.. ..	40
WORK AND REST	.. ..	42
VINCENT LEE : A TALE ..	.. ..	44
DIONYSUS	.. ..	53
THE LITTLE ONE'S REST	.. ..	56
THE MAIDEN'S LOST LOVE ..	.. .. ..	58
OTHER DAYS	.. ..	60
MAY	.. ..	62

CONTENTS.

	PAGE
A Birthday Festival	64
The Ring	66
The Ingle Nook	68
The Gardener	76
Evening	78
In Search of Truth	80
A Fragment	85
The Captain	86
To My Love	92
Larma	95
Adieu to Upper Thames	101
Boat Song	103
Ode to History	106
The Betrothal	111
Love's Cloud	113
An Awakening	115
Discovery of Earthly Love	122
In Search of Heavenly Love	124
Prince Imperial : In Memoriam	126
Bernard and Sylvia : A Duet	130
A Hymn	133
A Hymn	135
A Hymn	137
A Hymn	139
Agnes ; or the Hilly Path. A Tale	141
The Bower of Souls	178
Legend of the Moss Chapel	292

AGNES;

THE BOWER OF SOULS;

AND OTHER POEMS.

— ✿✿✿ —

FANCY.

—

As pure as the Lily,
  Sweet as the May,
As eve full as stilly,
  Closing the day,
Is Fancy when soaring,
  Dreaming away,
On Love ever poring,
  Whispering its lay.

So gentle its sighing,
  Lowly and calm
On high ever flying,
  Seeking a balm
Exalting our being,
  Bringing a tear,
Denying our seeing
  Ever a fear.

B

A ZEPHYR.

—

Oh ! could I be the balmy air,
  What sweetness would I kiss,
No luscious fruit, nor dewy bud,
  Would I in wandering miss.
      For me the breeze,
      Should roses seize,
And bring their perfume to the bower,
      Where lover's gay,
      Upon that day
Should feel the essence of my power.

My guide should be the butterfly,
  Wherefrom myself to load ;
E'en on my way forgetting not
  The honey bee's abode.
      To waft along
      A sylvan song,
To all who beauty were adoring,
      To Cupid's wing,
      From song birds bring
Their ecstacy when they were soaring.

Then hastening from the joyous sound.
  Of merry village chimes,
Far would I go, and burdened bring,
  Aromas from the scented climes,
    An ocean shell
    Would o'er the swell,
Bring safely buoyed my gathered spices,
    Which should be bound
    To hover round,
At fairies' mystic sacrifices.

Upon the hawthorn would I sit,
  Beside the quiet lane,
Nigh canopied with chestnut trees,
  Nor should I wait in vain.
    With birds above
    Beguiling love,
And saunterers all who might be roaming,
    To wander near
    The fragrance clear,
That culled I in the pleasant gloaming.

THE MERRY SONGSTERS.

—

Come, let us ramble near the streams,
 Rippling water pleases,
The air is warm with solar beams,
 Sweet with tempering breezes.
Oh ! what a gladdening day it is !
  Hark ! hear the merry songsters,
   Now twittering,
   Now chirruping,
   Sweetly, sweetly,
   Sweetly chirruping.

Oh ! let us hurry to the vale,
 'Neath the trees all towering,
Amongst them, scented woodbines trail,
 Shrubs of rose empowering.
Come thence to while the happy hour,
 And hear the merry songsters,
   Now twittering,
   Now chirruping,
   Sweetly, sweetly,
   Sweetly chirruping.

CUPID SCORNED.

Woe ! woe ! the wind is moaning,
   For Cupid's love is scorned,
And elves are now intoning
   How fays upon him fawned.

In Beauty's bower he wandered,
   Unbidden was he there ;
Yet ere he left he pondered—
   Its thraldom was so fair.

Sore wounded by rejection,
   To realms despairing hied ;
And sickened through dejection,
   He pined away and died.

THE HOLIDAY.

—

Oh ! here in the meadow a sunny day,
 Come troop ye, come run, come troop,
Oh ! come all ye children for sport and play,
 To laugh, or to call, or whoop.
   A ball, a ball, a ball,
   A scramble now for all ;
Now throw it again, while they haste away,
To skip and to jump with a glee to-day.

  Chorus—
 They sing and they laugh all o'er,
 As never they laughed before ;
But dreaming of gaiety, merriment there,
Enjoying so greatly the fun of the fair.

Oh ! come, all ye lads and ye lasses gay,
 Come troop ye, come run, come troop,
'Tis fair, and a bright little childrens' day,
 To laugh, or to call, or whoop.
   A dance, a dance, a dance,
   Give plain and fair a chance,
Of kisses so coy, but so sweet to pay,
While twirling and dancing with glee to-day.

Chorus—

They sing and they laugh all o'er
As never they laughed before ;
But dreaming of gaiety, merriment there,
Enjoying so greatly the fun of the fair.

Now, hark, they will sing their sweet roundelay,
  Come troop ye, come run, come troop,
And form a fair ring of the mounds of hay,
  Nor laugh ye, nor call, nor whoop.
        A song, a song, a song,
        Let silence joy prolong ;
Until in the chorus to join you may
With happiest voices with glee to day.

Chorus—

They sing and they laugh, etc.

For strawberries, buns, pretty cakes galore,
  Come troop ye, come run, come troop,
And rosy sweet lips all refreshed the more
  May laugh then, or call, or whoop.
        A race, a race, a race,
        Yet brightens each dimpled face,
But many now tumble and fall o'er the hay,
Too tired for more racing with glee to-day.

Chorus—

They sing and they laugh, etc.

Now gather ye girls and all boys in line,
　　Come troop ye, come run, come troop,
And bring all your things and your flowers fine,
　　Yet laugh ye, or call or whoop.
　　　　　　A ride, a ride, a ride,
　　　　　　Till home is fair espied ;
When each one shall tell their own tale and say,
What all here have done with such glee to-day.

　　　　CHORUS—
　　And slept they when sleep came o'er,
　　As never they slept before ;
All dreaming they were in that meadow down
　　there
Enjoying still greatly the fun of the fair.

EARLY DAWN.

Shining now, o'er half the sphere,
  Lending whilst receiving ;
Rivals to yon moon are near ;
  Triumph ne'er achieving.

Brilliant Beacon wander on,
  Pilot to the straying ;
Harbour to the lost, anon ;
  Never yet betraying.

Darkened is the face of night,
  Starry grandeur wearing ;
Clear and snowlike is the light,
  Earth and heaven sharing.

Nature seems awhile entranced,
  E'en though never resting ;
Beauties hourly are enhanced ;
  Industry suggesting.

Peaceful calmness hovers o'er,
　　Herald of the dawning ;
Blushing every moment more,
　　Smiling in the morning.

Brightening now is all around,
　　Gold ephemeral cheering ;
Many a sweet and transient sound,
　　Tells us day is nearing.

Full and blithesome is the heart,
　　Nature now admiring ;
Praise and worship be our part,
　　Never, never tiring.

Now yon skylark soars on high,
　　Cheering mates in rising ;
Hark ! the song is in the sky,
　　Man of morn apprising.

ANXIETY.

—

Acute the hearing, keen the wearied sight
   To catch at every sound and fancied stir
   Of little things, imagined to concur
With transient thought, that fevered in its might,
Is ofttimes checked while in its restless flight ;
   Confusing systems with the maddening whirr
   Of rushing errors ; which at first deter
The solving of the certain course of right,
And then will leave behind a troubled brain.
   If then our thoughts and wishes do not blend,
If then an hour's anxiety is pain.
   How soothing is the knowledge of the end !
A word may loose the rack, the tortuous strain,
   And sweetest hours of calm the soul attend.

THE HONEYSUCKLE.

—

Come now, tender, sweet woodbine, thy perfume's
     full power,
  As an offering to love and old memories dear ;
Let Affection's rich incense now cling round the
.   bower,
    To enchant with its fragrance the hearts that are
        near.
Let us call back the thoughts, and the scenes of
        the past,
  That remind us of pleasures that used to beguile,
And renew the old love that then bound us so fast
    With the warmth and the feeling that ushered
        a smile.

Let not all the fond hopes that were fostered yet
        fade,
  Nor the sorrows of old be e'er gathered again ;
Neither seek for the reason a parting was made,
    Nor recall the fell grief that o'ershadowed us
        then.
But endow every zephyr that passes with love,
    To be wafted on high from the dell to the air ;
By enriching the wavelets that soar far above
    We surround us with essences dainty and fair.

Nor the rose, nor the ivy we seek as a friend,
   For the one has a thorn, and the other a fang,
'Twill absorb and absorb till its victim shall bend,
   And around its own work like a parasite hang.
So, now come, oh, sweet woodbine, and cling as ye
      may ;
   Cling around with devotion, cling surely and
    well ;
For such bountiful love lends a glorious ray,
   And envelops the heart and the soul in its
    spell.

REST NOT.

—

Nature tells us not to weary,
   System orders no delay,
Weeds will make the pathway dreary,
   Be our active hands away.
Sunny rays are ever changing
   Places o'er the germs of life,
Round the planet ever ranging
   Shadows trail in endless strife.

Onward, onward, e'er increasing,
   Worldly progress year by year ;
Time runs backward, never ceasing
   Habit brings regret nor fear.
Clouds across the sky are driving,
   Somewhere moves the wind and gale,
Death means life, in myriads thriving ;
   Joy comes after Sorrow's wail.

Empire follows Empire falling,
   Nations rise where sets the sun,
Desert and morass recalling
   Cities that renown had won ;
It is Nature, though not seeming,
   Man but seeks a place to build—
Distant shores with wild birds teeming,
   With the nesting they are filled.

Lands are sinking, seas are spreading,
  Hills arise where shone the lake ;
Shrubs and trees anon are shedding
  What hereafter forests make.
Summer's fulness scarcely clearing,
  Nature takes another form ;
Mantling crystals white appearing,
  Covering, crowding, keeping warm.

Webs all broken and distended
  By the giddy flies at noon,
Are at night-time perfect mended,
  Flies are few beneath the moon.
Day by day the busy trappers
  View their fabrics tear and spoil,
Patiently, in green leaf wrappers—
  For a meal was all their toil.

Think, when booms the rolling thunder
  Through the might of flashing fire,
Earth and air then rent asunder,
  E'er to sit in wanton ire ?
Such, with grief, ambition, trouble—
  Glory in the battle's throe—
Thrust beside a bursting bubble
  To be cancelled with its blow.

Hive the bee and dress the larder,
   Scout the slothful and the drone,
Lest there come a time much harder,
   Lest attends but want alone.
Active be as restless swallow,
   O'er the lake and o'er the lea,
Hive the bee its life to follow—
   Times shall come when rest may be.

Yet remember youth may never
   Make the honoured claim to rest ;
Hoary is the trunk we sever
   Thus to sink on Nature's breast.
'Tis the aged past their toiling
   Are allowed an envied share,
Weakness their endeavours foiling ;
   Nature will no effort spare.

Matter drifted, heat adjusted,
   Elements yet beyond decay,
Granite, coal, and sand encrusted,
   Thatched again with chalk and clay.
With the very dust 'twas causing
   Saving winds have spread the field ;
Therefrom, Nature, never pausing,
   All the wants of life may yield.

Surging waters, moving masses,
  Unto goals, nor seen, nor known,
Formed, perhaps, from primary gases,
  Cutting a gorge through rock and stone.
Rests it, think ye, o'er the river?
  Rests it, think ye, o'er the sea?
Rests it, think ye, while we shiver
  O'er an earthquake's liberty?

Other worlds than ours revolving,
  Each around their mystic sun,
Offer problems for our solving
  Deeper as the ages run.
Yet, evolving, or creating,
  Whiche'er science makes its choice
It is certain there are waiting
  Hearts at beauty to rejoice.

So where'er thy idol finding,
  All excepting work of man,
Where thy treasure, there the binding;
  Let it be in Nature's span.
Call it Light, or call it Beauty,
  Maybe Virtue, Truth, or Power,
Recognised shall be our duty;
  God is worshipped in that hour.

A SACK OF FLOUR.

—

Now the boys from the schoolroom had rattled
    away,
  And the master had taken his frugal tea ;
He then gazed o'er the fields that in sunny array,
  By their smiling suggested a ramble free.

Strolling forth by the brooks on that beautiful eve,
  He sought way, by the which, he might teach
    next morn ;
As he always endeavoured a plan to conceive,
  Which would interest the boys of the village
    born.

Soon he met Samuel Miles of the farm in the lane,
  Who was bent on a chat, and a pipe and glass
At the Swallow close by. 'Twas as good for the
    grain
  To be toasted, as 'twas for a village lass.

" Ah, good e'en, Master Watts, and, now how is
    the bairn ?
For methinks he's a dunce and his master bad.
What d'ye say, Master Watts, can ye say he do
    lairn ?
For 'tis sure that too much 'tis I spend on lad."

" He is numbered the sixth in the fourth remove,
    His attendance is fair and his conduct good,
And a question full hard will his progress prove,
    Or ye try, or ye test, as a doctor would."

" Number six in the fourth remove," growled
    Miles,
    " Now what crop have I got in partition five,
In yon nine-acre field beyond the stiles,
    Can ye tell me ? nay, yet 'tis as plain as hive

        Of yon wiseacre lads
        In their school-form fads,
        In the fourth remove,
        But we'll progress prove.

For thou wantest a sack, of good flour a sack.
    Now I'll wager the sack as he sends it to thee.
He shall measure the sack, of good flour a sack,
    And whate'er thou receivest a sack it shall be.

Be it found he be right, thou shalt have it free;
　Be it found to be less, still a sack shall it be :
But for all there is o'er double pay to me :
　That my wager is fair, you, I think, must agree."

　　　" I agree it is fair
　　　And the offer is rare
　　　And I have not a care
　　　There'll be less or to spare."

And he parted from Miles with the matter
　　arranged,
　And he laughed to himself for the wit of it,
For it was but the fruits of a craft interchanged ;
　And a joke, not a bet—not a bit of it.

Surely certain was he that the laddie was bright,
　Surely certain he knew well his table book,
With his sums up to fractions invariably right.
　Did he reckon the fact of an overlook ?

How the boys all would laugh on the morrow's gay
　　morn,
　When he told them the tale of the floury cross,
And of never a word should the tale e'er be shorn,
　It would teach them the value of profit and loss.

Farmer Miles had his chat, and his glass, and went
   home,
   Then he called his son Tommy, and bade him
      expound,
The short measure of flour, and not hasten to
   roam,
   In the morning's sweet air, ere a sack he had
      bound.

" Well, four pounds to a quaärtern, four quaärterns
   a pearck,
And four pearcks to a bushel, four bushels a seark."
      This was what Tom said,
      As he scratched his head,
      Where he seemed to store
      All his figures four,
      Bringing one now by one
      In consecutive run,
      And perhaps by the hour
      Have applied to the flour,
      If he had not seen smiles
      Light the face of old Miles,
      Who then said it would do for the night,
      But took care not to say it was right.
      He then told him to rise with the dawn,
      And get ready a sack by the morn,

To be carried to Watts at the school,
Nor to measure it wrong like a fool,
But to give all the weight that was due ;
If not pressed in the one sack take two.

Tommy pondered that night upon what might be
    meant,
    Thought of catches and punishment near or in
        store.
Yet at length fell asleep in the sleep sweetly sent
    To a child's pretty eyes, but which brightens
        them more.

Then awakened at dawn to the barn bins he ran,
    And he measured the pounds and the quarterns
        and all,
But a sack he had not, so again he began
    To consider his tables, the measures recall.

He remembered the hint about sack number two,
    And was seeking the motive inducing the
        thought ;
So he emptied the sack to his labour renew,
    As a fresher idea hovered o'er and was caught.

Then said he, " It be five of the bushels to searck,
    Why, of coourse, I was thinking of four all along,

And two pearcks to the bushel, eight quaärterns to
    pearck ;
Why now, true, I'm an ass, on all fours am so
    strong."

    So with extra good care
    He then weighed out full fair
    All eight quarterns on top
    Of four pounds without stop.
    He thereon of fair pecks threw in two
    Marking well how the size of it grew,
    He soon wanted the other sack too,
    And felt sure that good Watts had his due,
    As he tied up their necks tight and fast,
    Having plumped in the five bushels last.

Farmer Miles's fair eyes then lit up with a smile,
    As 'ere sending to Watts he put sacks in the scale.
As a sack and a half it went down in true style,
    And he chuckled at Watts o'er his first morning's
    ale.

No amusing good tale went the school all around,
    For poor Watts wore a serious face all the day,
Little Tommy was punished each day it was found,
    And the measures unknown had to write and to
    say.

Then the neighbours would laugh, and the boys
    loudly call,
  " But a sack and a half, yet he pays for two."
" But a sack and a half," was oft seen as a scrawl,
    And the people who knew it not, soon were few.

When the farmer had had a good laugh and was
    paid,
    He called Tommy, and went to the barn again.
Tommy weighed a half sack now without any aid,
    It was sent round to Watts then by one of the
    men.

'Twas then Watts brightened up, and regained his
    old cheer,
    And the boys were once more all amused as of
    old.
'Twas a joke, not a bet, and good Miles was e'er
    dear
    As to masters, to pupils, and neighbours untold.

TO MAIDENS.

—

Come ! oh ! maidens list ! come, and I will sing
　　　To thee of love,
'Tis a tyrant bird, though e'en here and there
　　　A gentle dove ;
List, and learn to gain courteous lover dear
　　　With virgin art,
For a gleeful glance, and a dimpling smile
　　　Will warm his heart.

Let the smirk be coy, with a pretty pout,
　　　Thy shoulders shake,
Sigh he will and may, for his heart so proud,
　　　Oh, let him quake ;
So the trout takes bait, play and angle well
　　　Thy line draw in ;
Then enchant his ear with a pleasing voice,
　　　This grace will win.

So to whisper love he will come to thee,
  All silent thou,
Whilst all eager he, thou wilt him allow
  To kiss thy brow ;
With an upward look, and a gaze of love
  To make him fond,
Then a mutual kiss, and a close embrace
  Will seal the bond.

ANTOINE'S SONG.

IN BROKEN ENGLISH.

—

Now if ever again to dat sveet little place
   I might hopefully trace back my vay ;
Tis de village vhere Lelé for beauty and grace
   Over all oder lassies holds svay.
         C'est vrai, tra la la,
         C'est vrai, tra la la.

Yet she may have her suitors and rich may dey be,
   And myself e'en forgotten by name ;
But dough poor ven I left she a difference vould see,
   And she vould not be sorry I came.
         C'est vrai, tra la la. etc.

Oh : I tink I should find de same love as of yore,
   Her affection for me none de less ;
If I ask her to be to me just as before
   And to marry I tink 'twould be " Yes."
         C'est vrai, tra la la. etc.

THE ORPHAN.

—

Pity, oh ! pity the orphan maid
   Weeping now bitterly as she stands,
Where her dear mother in death is laid,
   Where now she prays with uplifted hands,

Recklessly rending her lonely soul,
   Sinking in grief to the selfish earth,
Timid of gaining the heavenly goal,
   Sobbing at thought of her mother's worth.

Silently pondering o'er the grave,
   Mournfully seeking consoling aid,
Memory master and mind the slave,
   Saddening tears was the tribute paid.

Homeward now wending her weary way,
   Calmly contented with heavenly care,
Knowing her mother had gone for aye—
   Gone to the rest of the good and fair.

HOPE.

Fair hope methinks is good unto the mind,
   Dispensing healthy tones to spirits low,
   Keeping a harmony of life to flow,
Our ken refreshing, though itself be blind.
To poor dejected senses it is kind,
   Whispering a promise more of weal than woe,
   Long terms of weary doubt all pass and go
As round our hearts the wreaths of hope we bind
The strength triumphant o'er the ills we feel
   Prepares our courage e'er against reverse ;
A seeming myth, but with a future real,
   It spreads a blessing o'er the universe.
It will hereafter prompt a soul's appeal
   And every care and baneful fear disperse.

THE MARCH OF LIFE.

—

Dauntless comrades now discover
What chaste passion firmly moves thee,
Parting brother, sister, lover,
What the furnace heat that proves thee.
Art of death all callous dreaming,
Dogged fighting, never caring?
Weapons all so brightly gleaming
In support of mythic daring.

CHORUS—
Brother, no; 'tis something nearer,
Fairer, sweeter, we are needing;
For the Word to us is clearer
That commands our joyous heeding,
Than to Death our march is dearer,
All for Life shall be our bleeding.
Ay, for Life.

Stalwart soldier now revealing
  High the brilliant standard crosses,
Where the braver, deeper feeling.
  Than is shown in Death's dark losses ?
Though the object be the rarer,
  Better good in highest seeking,
Canst possess a blessing fairer
  Than thy parent Earth's bespeaking ?

  Brother, there is something nearer, etc.

Keen the eye o'er distance glancing
  Marking foemen warriors trooping,
Battle scents the charger prancing
  'Side of man no spirit drooping.
How unfurling banners sparkling
  Bright reflect the sun-ray teeming,
Through the all-wide smoke cloud darkling
  Calmer Nature's peaceful beaming.

  Brother, there is something nearer, etc.

Clarion, drum, and bugle sounding,
  Drowning cries of pain and writhing ;
Strength repulsing, there rebounding,
  Death the tyrant double tithing.

Where the vaunted dream of glory
  O'er the sickening field and region,
Trampled deep in moisture gory
  Where in horror sleeps a legion?

    Brother, there is something nearer, etc.

Stand ye ready, comrades, ready,
  Higher raise the cross-like spangle,
Here is Death's white steed, oh! steady,
  Throw the charge back, rise and mangle.
Victory, ah! falls he stricken,
  Victory o'er this great anguish,
Shall he never, never quicken,
  Or in torments ever languish.

    Brother, there is something nearer, etc.

Sin's great battle o'er for ever,
  Life triumphant reigns in glory.
Death in sin from Life shall sever,
  Life in death shall aye be hoary.
Sweet this Liberty and surely
  Death is death, and chains and wailing.
Liberty seeks death not purely,
  For it e'er should Life be hailing.

    Brother, this is something nearer, etc.

Sing the march of Life, oh, brother,
    Homeward as our feet are wending,
Let not wife, nor father, mother,
    Sorrow seize from sorrow trending.
Measure steps with purer singing,
    Measure Life by a righteous living;
And the sum will be the bringing
    Of a soul to the Spirit-giving.

        Brother, this is something nearer, etc.

Home at last and welcome flowing
    From the dear ones now all vieing,
Eagerly their love-thought showing
    By their present crowded hieing.
Hail to Life, and all returning,
    Hail to Life, and all the sleeping,
Countless angels now are yearning
    Deep to gather them in keeping.

        Brother, this is something nearer, etc.

SPRING.

—

Awaken, sweet spirit of Earth,
　The sun is now warming thy heart!
Pour forth what thou storest of worth,
　Give out of thy treasures a part.
Display thy gem Beauty, O, Spring!
　Spread o'er the dark land thy fresh green!
Let winds scatter seed on the wing
　To clothe it in glorious sheen.

Arouse thee, and shake off thy sloth!
　Come, throw off thy dust quilt and frost!
Come, hark thee, and quicken all growth
　So yearned for ere sun-rays be lost.
Burst out of thy flint-coats, ye seeds!
　Uplift your bowed heads to the sky!
Then drink ye the dew honeyed beads
　And warmth that is shed from on high.

Sun ! brighten the skeleton forms,
  And dress the gaunt trees now all bare.
Thy heat draws the sap and then warms
  The branches and golden buds fair.
Oh, Spring ! let thy life flow with balm !
  Give splendour and joy for awhile !
Let, let the old Earth wear a charm,
  And cheer its old face with a smile.

AUTUMN.

—

Fulfilled is the promise of Spring !
  How grand is the beauty around !
How thankful all hearts when they bring
  The harvest all gleaned from the ground !
O, Autumn ! yet cast not the leaf
  From oak, beech, nor elm, ere we take
Full joy of thy blandishments brief,
  'Tis hard from thy glory to break.

Green shrub, moss, and heather in bloom,
  In clearing, in copse, and in glade
Are sweet to the eye from the gloom
  O' the woodland's o'er arching cool shade.
The bracken, the bramble, and birch
  Tell surely of freedom and grace ;
And woodbine repays for the search
  When kisses come back in its place.

Ah ! see how the yellows and browns
   Predominate far o'er the lea ;
All red gold or olive those crowns,
   Those dresses of shrub and of tree.
What going to die ?   Shall we mourn ?
   Such grandeur to die.   Shall we weep ?
Nay, 'tis but to rest until dawn—
   Till Spring again comes they must sleep.

GOLD.

—

I threw a little fair-haired boy
  Some bright and golden coin ;
And knelt I down 'mongst many a **toy,**
  So in the play to join.
More cared he for the noisy tray
  Than what then glittering rolled ;
And his indifference made me say
  I would I knew not gold.

Oh, let me have the happy smile,
  And childhood's days come back ;
Returning to those joys awhile,
  The innocence I lack.
No care for money, nor its use,
  Commanding boons untold,
The having it begets abuse,
  I would I knew not gold.

List ! to the songsters in the morn,
   The breaking bud of day.
Their songs upon the breezes borne
   Receive no gilded pay.
They on the boughs no slavery know
   But wings of freedom fold,
Then I will sing my carol so—
   I would I knew not gold.

MY LOVE.

—

I sing a lay unto her eyes
  Both beautiful and blue,
And praises oft upon her hair
  All of a golden hue.
Her form so fine, no bosom soft,
  Ere rose and fell more pure,
I could not from her brightness dwell,
  Without her love endure.

Her presence like the full blown rose
  Lends perfume all around,
Her footsteps have a majesty
  And queenly mark the ground.
She meets one as the sunny spring,
  With bursting radiance clear,
Retiring as the autumn does,
  E'er leaving memories dear.

erghttysnsed.

Yet not too fine for kindly words,
 Nor charity too proud,
Her mind and all her sylph-like form
 With virtue is endowed.
So if she be an angel here,
 Accepting worldly love,
How prized her soul must be on high,
 'Mongst seraphs far above.

WORK AND REST.

—

Oh, Genevieve ! come sit beside,
　The day has told its hours full long,
Enough thy busy hands have tried,
　Come sit and mark the thrush's song,
We men may work with sturdy arm,
　And hard and heavy it may be,
But when the sun may no more charm,
　We love to rest, and why not thee.

Nay, nay.　A woman's work ne'er done !
　Come here, and nestle close to me ;
If I say rest, loved little one,
　Why ; let the work unfinished be.
I want to tell thee what I thought
　While at my labour all the day,
And how thy fond sweet love has wrought,
　And how o'er all it held its sway.

My arm was stronger, head more clear
To wrestle with the task and strain,
For thou wert there and made it dear,
And easier for the end to gain.
And now 'tis o'er, our day is done,
Let you and I contented kiss ;
For He who set the hours to run
Meant not to leave no time for bliss.

VINCENT LEE.

—

FIT I.

Now list ! and I a tale will tell
　All as 'twas told to me,
And how it came and how it fell
　About one Vincent Lee.
Who journeyed to the country side
　Far, far, away to see,
And with his father's friend to bide,
　A good old squire was he.

Right welcome was young Vincent made,
　When he arrived down there,
And rich the board before him laid
　For eager youth to share.
He lingering gazed on maiden sweet,
　As fair he ne'er had seen,
As Louie Neale, who came to meet
　Their guest with modest mien.

For miles around was Louie known
   And loved by every one,
Full proud the sire's heart to own
   That she such love had won.
Good were the tales the neighbours told
   Which he rejoiced to hear,
And, thankful, down there often rolled
   The semblance of a tear.

Now Louie all their rambles led
   And he all willing viewed,
While o'er the hills and meads they sped,
   The gems fair nature strewed.
They gaily traced the widening brook
   Which crossed the opening glade,
And then would seek a pleasant nook
   To rest within its shade.

They lightly in the flowery dell
   Would in the gloaming stroll
Until through charming fancies fell
   A lulling o'er the soul.
For Nature sweetly bounds the heart
   Instilling quiet peace,
When sympathy may breathe a part
   All thoughts of trouble cease.

At eve the song rang through the hall
   And homely mirth would reign,
Until the powers of night would fall
   Ascendancy to gain.
Refreshed by rest, at opening day
   They to the stream would go,
And ample breakfast bring away
   With each a healthful glow.

And thus he came to love and woo
   The lovely Louie Neale,
For Love's return he oft would sue,
   Yet none could Louie feel.
Still time, he thought, would surely tell,
   And cause her love to flow,
For time will often break the spell
   Of such indifference slow.

Now many a day had so passed by
   And Vincent was to leave
The house and all its haunts so nigh
   At which he could but grieve.
Oh! That a happy farewell stroll
   With Louie by his side
Could gain an answer to console
   A hope ere now denied.

He hailed a last excursion then
   The squire one eve proposed,
To take the boat down stream again
   As far as hills enclosed.
They near the falls arrived would see
   Him angling as they came,
And if 'twere fine, the morn would be
   Fair auspice of their aim.

The hours of night passed slowly by,
   For Vincent restless lay,
Impatient for the brightening sky
   To soon declare it day.
Ere long it came with joyous song,
   And all was fresh and gay,
The gates were opened with a throng
   Of angels in each ray.

FIT II.

A pretty craft was seen to glide
   Forth gently from the shore,
And pleasantly the oars were plied
   Ne'er plied so well before.
Sweet Louie sat then in the stern
   And Vincent in the fore,
Yet marked he well each point and turn
   While down the stream they bore.

Sublimely grand the picture drawn,
   The weird and distant hills
In warm transparent shadows borne
   Down o'er the lake and rills.
While here the glittering stream received
   The likeness of a view
Of varied scenes above perceived,
   A sky of every hue.

And presently he gently spake
   Of love with ardent voice,
And sought to know if aught could make
   Him worthy of her choice.
Persuasive tones as soft and kind
   As e'er a maiden heard
Were thrown, alas ! upon the wind,
   Nigh lost was every word.

Still slowly came the answer firm,
   Though yet her heart was free,
Be short or long to wait the term
   In vain it would all be.
No explanation could she give—
   Where is the maid that can ?
Enough for her to wish to live
   The life already ran.

Oh ! tell me why his face so changed
    Which erst with kindness teemed,
But now to ashen dulness ranged
    A very fiend he seemed.
May envy fill the mortal frame
    While malice struts behind ?
Then wonder not that hatred came
    To fill a little mind.

Now smoothly, smoothly, drifting on,
    Unconsciously too near,
The scene around they gazed upon
    Beguiled them from all fear.
They heard no angler's warning shout
    Against the falls below,
Too far the current bore them out,
    Against which none could row.

Ah ! who could think that Vincent knew
    The villain's part now played,
That he who once so ardent grew,
    Had to a snare betrayed.
But so the tale—to frighten one
    Was all perhaps was meant ;
Control he lost, the evil done,
    And to the brink they went.

E

Mark! how the angry torrents pour,
   A fount of showery spray,
As several streams uniting roar
   Like lions in the fray.
Down the abyss they thundering go,
   In fury seem to boil,
And fairy forms and grottoes shew
   Ere resting from their toil.

Above the falls there stood a tree
   That stretched its branches o'er,
He knew to grasp them well might he
   So save the boat once more.
Though chief the thought himself to save
   From peril now ahead,
There Louie sat as calm, as brave,
   While never a word was said.

The scene was wild as rugged broke
   The rocks athwart the stream,
The boat rushed on, 'midst crashing stroke
   Received on beam and beam.
But near the brink it whirled around,
   The stern towards the bank;
'Twas then young Vincent fiercely frowned,
   From thought of death then shrank.

Now quickly Louie grasped the tree
　　The boat had brought her near,
She then close by her sire could see
　　Fast hurrying down in fear.
For very life young Vincent tried
　　To gain the branch, but no,
He leapt a leap by far too wide,
　　And then was dashed below.

Then soon a father's careful arm
　　Assisted to the bank,
Brave Louie, safely from alarm,
　　And on his breast she sank.
Though distant he had seen the whole,
　　And hastened to the place,
He knew the waters had control,
　　Yet ran the futile race.

He saw the stern whirl round about,
　　He saw her gallant spring,
And also Vincent leaping out—
　　Indeed a desperate thing.
He would not say it was deserved :
　　The end young Vincent met :
Too thankful Louie was preserved,
　　His own and only pet.

How real imagination grows
　And tragic fancies seem
When night in slumber eyelids close,
　And thoughts of others teem.
The morn it came, and Louie woke
　As light began to gleam,
Around she gazed, and smiling spoke,
　Convinced 'twas all a dream.

DIONYSUS.

—

Oh ! come, ye nymphs, and dance along,
Let merry joy create the song,
And here and there the cymbals clash.
All tuned to harmonise the crash.
Ye bright-eyed maidens gaily dance,
And with your smiles with joy entrance
Attending gods and love-sick swains,
Then give them wine to ease their pains,
Sileni, Pans, and satyrs come
And tune your reeds when maids are dumb.

Now hail ! glad Dionysus, hail !
Let naught the festive mirth assail,
For see the clustering grapes are wound
The jovial god's fair brow around.
And there a train of sylphs appear,
The cone-topped thyrsus mingles near
All borne by virgins laurel-wreathed,
Just fluttered by the zephyr breathed ;
Now mark the sacred things they bring
And in procession gladly sing.

The tuft-eared lynx first takes the lead,
The docile ass next treads the mead,
The surly panther, head erect,
Is fain to sing, would gods direct.
To hail this bright, this sunny day,
Sweet birds now herald in the play.
A floral chain, sufficient check,
Entwined about a tiger's neck,
That now, submissive, bows its head,
Full proud to be so gently led.

The flowers choice that strew the sheen
Lend perfume to the joyous scene.
And ivy, laurel, asphodel,
Enticing bees from honeyed cell,
Bedeck the sacrificial ram,
Led forth e'en as a peaceful lamb
By damsels singing cheerily,
And dancing, dancing merrily,
Come some from Macedonian dell,
From Attica the throng they swell.

Mimallones and Thyades,
Though frantic, skip in graceful ease,
And Maenades with more combine
To wreath themselves with luscious vine,
The curling snake in honour placed ;
For sacred held, 'tis not debased.

And garlands rich, festooned are seen
From female hands to hang between.
So fitly gay, the pageant bright,
Beguiling both the mind and sight.

Come fays to serve the goblet round,
Whilst featly tripping o'er the ground.
Oh, drink to Ariadne fair,
The balmy purpling liquid there ;
Nor let these orgies have an end,
But with bacchantic revels blend
The worship of the Grace's three.
So quaff now to Euphrosyne,
Thalia and Aglaia too,
And give them all the honour due.

Oh, hark ! the heart's pure music sounds,
And with it how the glade resounds,
E'en from the groves the echo clear
Falls sweetly on the listening ear.
Such praise from earthly beings' voice
With such delights, make gods rejoice.
The eager shepherds gather near
To join the gala and the cheer,
And dance and sing in praise of wine,
Of Dionysus and the vine.

THE LITTLE ONE'S REST.

A few verses on viewing a friend's child asleep.

—

Sleep, oh ! sleep.   Life's peace is short,
  A long, long time, oh ! guileless be,
While many in vain for rest exhort
  May Morpheus wave his wand o'er thee.
Thy rosy lip, all tempting curve,
  Alike thy little closed blue eye,
Discover neither throb nor nerve,
  So animation seems to lie.

Oh ! offspring of true happiness,
  On which the gifts of love attend,
May Heaven's love and holiness
  Full graciously on thee descend.
Thou art proud man in infancy,
  But e'en with scarce incipient power,
All guiltless of delinquency ;
  A bud to ope a pretty flower.

So purely now are moonbeams shed
    That even shadows seem to shine,
Oh ! be the paths as fair to tread
    What time in life thy steps incline.
Oh ! gently press thy downey nest
    Till wakening eyes declare the dawn,
Till birds shall wake thee from thy rest,
    And sunlight peeps through curtains drawn.

New thoughts of children and of men
    Came trooping past in quick array,
Many a thought came o'er me then
    That, yet, I know remains to-day.
How beautiful it looked to me
    As it was calmly lying there ;
So calmly, aye, 'twas heaven to see,
    Humanity without a care.

THE MAIDEN'S LOST LOVE.

—

The eagle kens the mountain side,
    And builds its home,
The seagull skims the ocean tide,
    And sips its foam.
So merrily shines the sparkling wave,
    That crests the deep,
But naught doth mark my lover's grave.
    Where I may weep.

My soul, oh ! let me follow him ;
    My early love.
I watch, and watch—my eyes are dim,
    Come back my love !
Nay, nay, the waters hush my cry,
    And secret keep ;
To lead my fancies passing by,
    Where I may weep.

The night is come, and yonder star
    Now seems to call ;
Now hoary clouds distend afar
    A darkening pall.
I hail thee, death ! I go where he
    My heart doth keep,
On him to lay my head, and be
    Where I may weep.

OTHER DAYS.

—

There are days we pass o'er with a smile,
  There are days we recall with a sigh,
There are times we are wont to beguile
  With the searching of memory's eye.
There are golden and silver ones there,
  Some of sunshine dark clouds come across ;
But the darker and stormy we ne'er
  When forgotten, e'er count as a loss.

Why not take, then, the days that were good
  As the kind to be followed for aye ?
But we cannot, alas, if we would,
  There are so many blocks in the way.
For, when bright and surrounded with wealth,
  When at word all fair blessings respond,
If no evils attend upon health,
  Yet one's soul yearns for something beyond.

Let them come then, and go as they may,
    The dull rain, fierce wind, or bright sun ;
Whether clear, whether stormy, or gay,
    All as long as our duty is done.
Soon the goal will then be within reach,
    In those days we no more shall despond,
Happy times to be loved, and when each
    Shall enjoy what was yearned for beyond.

MAY.

—

How sweetly the pretty birds sing,
  This merry May morn.
How spritely they flit on the wing,
  All airily borne.
See yonder the blossoming bell,
  Shy, bowing with dew,
The glistening glow of the dell
  Refreshed all anew.

Come quickly, bestir thee my boy!
  Out, out to the fields!
Go, gain from the air the full joy,
  The bloom that it yields.
Come rosy-cheeked sister join hands
  And dance to the sound,
Of music thine own, and in bands
  Wreath blossoms around.

When young how we wish to be old,
　When old to be young.
From breezes so loved by the bold
　A moan is oft wrung.
But dance will I now like a child
　Or run to a mark.
Glad voices, this morn fresh and mild,
　Shall sing with the lark.

Oh, oh, the fresh air, the sweet air !
　What spirit it lends
The weakly alike to the fair ;
　What tinting it blends.
So cheeringly breathe it, and sing
　Like birds this May morn,
And flowers all various bring,
　Sweet home to adorn.

A BIRTHDAY FESTIVAL.

—

Gaily dancing,
Joy enhancing,
Merrily singing,
Verily bringing
Glad mirth to the hearth and home.
Manly faces,
Female graces,
Bright eyes beaming,
Hearts all teeming
With love for the hearth and home.

Old folks' stories,
Children's glories,
Old age mingling,
Sex not singling,
With youth at the hearth and home.

Gladsome greeting,
Festive meeting,
Frowns eschewing
Smiles ensuing,
'Mongst friends at the hearth and home.

Fill the measure,
Hail all pleasure,
Sorrow sinking,
Toast now drinking
" The pride of the hearth and home."
She the dearest,
To them nearest,
Gather round her,
Love has crowned her,
The Queen of the hearth and home.

F

THE RING.

—

My love she knows not where I am,
　　Yet wonders.
My love she knows not how I love,
　　Yet wonders.
My love she knows not how I think
　　Of her now,
My love she knows not what I bring
　　To her now.

Oh ! I will tell her how I walked
　　Alone here,
So lightly 'neath the sparkling star
　　Alone here.
Yon gem of light shall be my love
　　Whilst from her,
And she shall be my heaven's star
　　When with her.

But what I bring I will then tell
To no one.
For she shall be of all who know
The first one.
So question not, I care no more
To linger,
I anxious am to place it on
Her finger.

THE INGLE NOOK.

—

"O remind me no more," he said,
  "O remind me no more,
Take the sad world away instead,
  With its wearisome lore.
I want nothing to do with it,
  Therefore take it away,
Nor to see, nor to hear a whit—
  There is nothing to say.
Let me rest in my ingle nook,
Let me rest in my ingle nook.
        Alack-a-day
        We wear away.
Shall ever we find a rest ?
        O yea, O yea,
        There come a day
When weary ones all may rest.

I have fought and have struggled of yore,
   And have worked with a will ;
Till my hands, feet and back have been sore,
   Yet have laboured while ill,
      On and on
      Thereupon
   A good fifty year.
      Yet with heart
      And no part
    Of unthrifty fear,
Did I garner a saving of gold
'Gainst the days that have come ; I am old.
     And infirmity waits
     By the grave's hollow gates,
     But I carry my head
     With proud step and firm tread,
   Full erect to the living and bold.
     Let me rest,
     Let me rest,
    With my pipe and book.
     Let me rest,
     Let me rest,
    In my ingle nook.

There is mother and I yet, my lass,
   All the others, thy brothers, have gone
To the field or the grave now, alas !
   'Twill be mine or the mother's anon.

O yea, O yea,
There come a day
When weary ones all may rest.
Do you think, lass, the little now left
For a comfort to mother or me,
Or, again, for yourself when bereft,
What may buy a few ribbons for thee,
May be squandered 'mong beggars and folk?
They should rather themselves and their shame
Hide away and afar, in the smoke
Of a town, than a village of fame
For a good honest name
Without blemish nor blame.

Note the disparity
Coming to thee,
Good as can be,
Seeking for charity.
No, remind me no more," he said,
" Remind me no more.
Take the sad world away instead,
With its wearisome lore.
What if she were
A cousin to thee?
Surely I swear
'Tis nothing to me.

Let her seek him who took her from hence,
  Or home where in separate place,
If she be not bereft of her sense,
  She would stay for an interval's grace.
But for me there is nothing to say,
  I want nothing to do with their cares.
Take the world and its burdens away,
  I can carry my own, but not theirs.
      And I take
      At the world
        Not a single look,
      For the sake
        Of my world
      And my ingle nook."

" O, come, close not thine heart," Alice said,
  " To a cry of distress, father dear.
Dost remember Elijah was fed
  By the woman, who more had to fear
Than the loss of a comfort or so ?
  If we follow the world as it leads
We shall come to a much greater woe,
  Than by showing it something it needs.
      Where the disparity
        Coming to me,
        Good as I be,
      Seeking for charity ?

There is one that yet might be implored,
The good Lord she at one time adored ;
  For that we are too good,
  It must be understood,
To be asked for the neighbourly dole.
   Oh, O oh, oh, O oh,
   Do not let me yet go.
   O father, no no,
   Let it never be so
Than ye prove thee a generous soul."

   "Yet," quoth he,
" Let me rest in my ingle nook.
   Let it be,
Let me rest in my ingle nook."

It was then gentle Alice arose
  And came round to her father and said,
" You but speak of my brothers. Why those,
  And yet never of Liz ?   Is she dead ?
Have you heard not a word since she went
  Over seas ?   Was she married away ?
Or did sister not seek your consent ?
  Why not tell me, dear father ? Come, say."

   But old Ronald looked stern,
   And his brow 'gan to burn

With a fire that was fierce,
While his eyes seemed to pierce
His fair questioner's face,
E'en as though he would trace
Of her meaning the course,
And, still further, its source.
Yet he saw there no guile ;
Then it lulled him to smile.
    And, quoth he,
    " Let it be,
    Ask me no more.
    I told ye before
I want nothing to do with it,
Nor to say, nor to hear a whit.
Let me rest in my ingle nook,
Let me rest in my ingle nook.
    Alack-a-day
    We wear away,
Shall ever we find a rest ?
    O yea, O yea,
    There come a day
When weary ones all may rest.

Here, beside me, my lass, now sit down,
    And come read to me out of the Book.
It will cheer us.   The world makes us frown,
    Like the breeze on the face of a brook."

Soon our Alice was there as he bade,
   Though her heart was nigh bursting for thought
How to speak, how to urge, or persuade
   Her loved father to grant what she sought.

She then read of forgiveness and peace,
   Of the debtors, and similar themes ;
Till at last the old man bade her cease,
   Being filled with more brightening gleams.
         And such promises fair,
         As were often told there,
       Than the world can e'er shew,
       Ever deal, ever know,
       His good heart seemed to melt.
       It was then, Alice felt
That the time had arrived to speak out ;
And she said without tremor or doubt,
        " Yea, O yea,
        Come a day
     When weary ones all may rest.
        Where no sin,
        Nor world's din
     Exists among angels blest."

Then she knelt there, her father beside,
   And she said, " O, my father, 'tis not
My young cousin I told answer to bide
   For your succour at grannie's old cot ;

It is Lizzie come back
O'er the ocean's long track.
And I know, and I know,
All there is e'er to know."

Then old Ronald arose, and he cried,
 " Is it true that our Lizzie is back ?
Then at grannie's no more shall she hide.
 My hat. Come, though the night be pitch black
        Come Alice, quick,
        My hat and stick ;
        Alack-a-day,
        We wear away,
    Shall ever we find a rest ?
    There's no rest in my ingle nook,
    There's no rest in my ingle nook.
        But yea, O yea,
        There come a day
When weary ones all shall rest."

THE GARDENER.

—

I turn the earth over
  To nourish its cells,
With roots of the clover,
  Sweet grass and bluebells.
I throw up the daisies,
  Dead leaves make good loam,
The worm from its mazes
  May seek a new home.

My arm is not weary,
  My foot is not cold,
Nor irksome, nor dreary,
  My toil on the mould.
And when the clod crumbles
  Its fragrance is mine,
So grateful, it humbles
  My heart at its shrine.

Man turns the world over
   For plants and their stems,
Becomes a far rover
   In seeking its gems ;
But this all my pleasure,
   Content of my toil,
The all of my treasure,
   The turn of the soil.

EVENING.

—

All o'er the homestead rest now reigns,
    No sound awakes the quiet round,
All save the cricket in the lanes
    Hath hushed its joyous daily sound.
Yon cottage tells of happy time,
    Of lowly comfort and content,
Of hearts that gladden at the chime
    When on their hardy toil intent.

With flowers trained through lattice fine,
    Convolvulus and woodbine sweet,
That each for simple love entwine
    And seem to kiss when blossoms meet
No wind to stir their lighter leaves,
    As Nature breathes but far above,
The marten nestles 'neath the eaves,
    And emulates domestic love.

Oh, would the darkness stay awhile
    Ere yet it hide the homely scene,
Which, free from discord as from guile,
    Is as the flowers upon the sheen :
But now it closes o'er the fields,
    Alike around the cot and me,
  nd as unto it twilight yields
      cry " Good night and peace to thee."

IN SEARCH OF TRUTH.

—

Is truth so rare, the false so rife
   That even yet the question old
Of what Truth is, still haunts proud life
   With sphynx-like heaviness untold ?
Time comes like feet of stinging fly,
   And thought is quick to grasp its weight ;
An instant more 'tis flitting by,
   And truth is lost, our vision late.

Erst wont to think that truth was seen,
   Or tasted, smelt, or heard, or felt,
Examined I these senses keen
   To find through which its medium dealt.
The special four, subjected first,
   But laid a snare for common lore ;
Yet, sure, I felt, the truth would burst
   From that more common sense in store.

I scanned the fields, the trees, the sky,
  The sun and stars, and all below,
Yet what we name the things on high
  But wordy semblance is, we know.
The cloud nor black, the sky nor blue,
  The trees rude bark, a false veneer.
Extending fields of varied hue,
  Like liars smile in covert sneer.

Fragmental ore, or hardy rock
  Of old-world fish composed—or wood,
Is ash of burnt-up time to mock
  The seeker of a truer good.
In homely life again I sought
  True thing, true flesh, true face, to find ;
Alas ! I looked, but found I nought,
  But while I looked became I blind.

Yet could I not still smell the fruit
  Of lemon, pine, and orange sweet,
The fragrant bloom or noisome brute,
  The odour of a dainty meat ?
The dish was foul, as foul could be,
  But food of fiend in any hell ;
The flowers and fruits but chemistry
  And next I lost the sense of smell.

G

No sight, nor smell, yet taste was there ;
    I epicurean choice retained ;
And loved the flavour of the rare,
    Nor from the ruddy wine refrained.
What then my horror once full tired,
    When faint and thirsting, I in haste,
Quaffed acid for the wine desired,
    And which destroyed all sense of taste.

All false, all false, false limbs, false eyes ;
    Ay, many parts of human frame
Lie down at night, at morning rise
    As false as all their owner's aim.
O, what an artificial sphere
    Here hangs in the air ; a bubble fair
Of bright reflected colours clear !
    Bah, it is gone.   O world ! beware !

Cannot I hear a bird of song ?
    Nothing false there.   Yea, 'tis a clock.
The sweet church bells their chimes prolong ?
    Nay, but a tiresome organ crock.
Comes there a voice of friend I know,
    Counsel of love, with honest brief ;
Alas, no friend draws near thee so,
    'Tis but a roaring braggart thief.

Hear ye the rain ? nay, 'tis not rain ;
　　'Tis but the wind o'er rustling leaves.
Ah, 'tis the wind, the same old strain,
　　Heralding e'er the lie it weaves.
Good heavens ! What shock so thrills mine ear ?
　　Thunder ? Or quakes the depths profound ? '
By tested guns I wandered near,
　　And lost for aye, all sense of sound.

Yet daunted not, of sense bereft,
　　Except the common one of touch ;
A nerve attracting warp and weft
　　Entrapping net for muscle-clutch.
I leaned contented and at rest
　　At thought of Truth within my grasp ;
It was the last, but greatest test :
　　A staff close-hugged within my clasp.

Though Esau's raiment and escheat
　　Came strongly forward to my mind,
Round curious Thomas no deceit
　　Nor falser, baser thought entwined.
But what a fall the chained-up strength,
　　Or confidence in petted dream,
May have when strained its utmost length,
　　And snaps it at the great extreme.

G—2

How faithfully I touched a stone ;
   As quickly crumbled it to dust.
The things I knew long years mine own
   Had changed, decayed, by rot and rust.
At last a limb, my flesh of life,
   That loved I in conceited youth,
When touched was dead, and cold to strife ;
   And soon I died, but then found Truth.

A FRAGMENT.

—

We little think ourselves unkind,
  When busy hands may break
The sweeter blossoms that we find
  Beside the rosy way we take.
E'en so let Nature share her own,
  Nor envy when she may desire
To place a dear one by her throne,
  With pride her bosom to inspire.

THE CAPTAIN.

—

Our lives and their peculiarities,
Their trials and many tempers, oft excite
An interest in them, both intense and great,
Compassion, unto indignation sore
And oftentimes amusement.   Nature shows
An ever-varying scene, so thought may tire,
Not in its voyage through its world, nor
Become insane whilst pondering o'er the few.
Diversity is the buoy of hope.   Hope's constant
        wing
Leaves in its flight all weariness behind,
To its own darksome misery.
                            This I found
Whilst travelling even o'er the ocean tracks ;
There would my speeding bark with seeming life
At times dance gaily o'er the waves, and then
The sea in fretful calm would make it still

In abject melancholy. Times as these
Would I in my experience lead the crew
And passengers to entertain their hearts
By goodly intercourse, of such a kind
As to withhold the outward matter free
From closer contact with the mind ; thereby
We gained enlightenment and gaiety,
So useful in dispelling care and all
The train of subtile thought that first may lead
Unto it. Heard I histories manifold
Told of themselves and things inanimate,
Of relatives and friends, both old and young,
That, like the atoms in a sunbeam, came
From out their places in the secret mind
To be enlightened by the confidence
Of social man. Hear one that comes to me
By present memory. The gay and good,
But mostly faces full of thought seemed all
To interest me.

      Wishing something done
Of moment but of daring, scarcely one
Would do, a man of sullen countenance
Once volunteered to execute the work
Required ; and, reckless in his movements, soon
Accomplished it ; from conversation long
With him in after hours I gathered this
His tale.

"From youth," said he, " I mixed with vice ;
A child I saw my father playing cards ;
A boy and man I saw him gaming still
I grew to like the play, and never checked,
I led a gambler's life until I loved :
'Twas then the fickle charm all slowly died
Away. I gamed no more. On passed the years,
In married bliss, and children grew around.
Good fortune smiled on industry, and gave
Us comfort, 'till a night of hell disturbed
Our peace. An old acquaintance sent to me
Friendly requests to come and dine with him ;
Cursed was the hour I went. Why did I go ?
Is there not something leading us at times ?
A destiny to err, or is the mind
So frail that Hell's own glittering tinsel wand
Can fascinate beyond control ?   I know
Not what it was, but went, and there I met
A number I had known before. But still
Feeling secure in much reserve, I mixed
In pleasantry with all ; cards were brought out,
By courtesy I joined. The cloth of silk
And gold that Satan strews the miry path
Towards his haunts with, causes one to fall
In darkness of impetuosity
O'er ruin's brink. The old excitement crept
Upon me, play ran high, I lost, I won,

And won and lost, with wine was heated, swore,
And staked my all—and lost.   I looked around ;
My fancy saw on every tongue the wish
To call me fool.

                 'Twas from that time began
My woe, my friends despised me, and every
    trial
I made to gain back fortune failed ; our home
Was broken up, so we might go to live
In some mere squalid den.   My children there
Became infected with disease, and five
Poor little things were laid beneath the sod
Within as many weeks.   Oh ! how I see
Their pretty faces now, with healthy cheeks
All gay and cheerful, knowing nought of woe,
As one would say, ' I like the old home best,'
And asked me, ' Why we came to live in such
A wretched place ? "   Oh ! how my heart then
    swelled
To think that I had caused it.   Hushing them
To silence, they would look and wonder, then
Would turn on merry heel, forgetting all
By happy childhood, all that troubled them.
How maddening that I lost them !   Little hearts !
Could I recall the past !   Upbraiding me
My wife there left me.

                                      Wandering, I knew
Not where, to seek her, yet I found her not.
Arriving at the port wherefrom your ship
Has come, I wavered.   Should I leave the land
Of birth, the land of kith and kin, to breathe
A new and fresher life afar ?   A month
Had passed, and still I asked myself the same.
At length with force the answer came to me,
Determined, desperate, go I would ; for though
I had not been all that I should have been
My wife had left me, throwing back the old,
Engaged responsibility ; so now
In taking that I go in search alone
For that I want, and in another sphere ;
For life I care not, let me risk it how
I may, where danger is 'tis there I go.
With love and friendship lost, why need I care ?
No, no, I go, and death shall be the bourn,
Rest and peace for a weary life, nor sought
Nor cared for."

                              Spoke he desperately ; when
I asked him, " If, supposing he should meet
His wife where he was going, then would each
Forget the past and try the world again
Together ? " Which he answered, saying " No,
No, never more, for ever parted now."

This stage of the recital gained, we all
Were startled by a piercing shriek, as through
A person's fright in falling overboard,
Full loud and sudden, then as quickly hushed.
Melting upon the waters—giving pain
To manly hearts, yet paralysing all
Our action.
                    Yet a moment and our brave
Companion dashed astern and over—soon
Appearing on the surface he was seen
To grasp a figure, then was heard a cry
Triumphant ; and he brought on board his wife.
For invalided she the voyage long
Had only come on deck that day in health
So soon to fall and fail again, but " Saved,
Saved, Saved !" was all our friend was heard to
        say.
All were surprised and pleased to know that one
Had found his wife and saved her ; in an hour
Retrieved the past, thanked Heaven, and loved
        again.

TO MY LOVE.

—

As from a dream I seem to wake
   Yet no alarm, nor ruder start,
The accents soft I hear now make
   Emotion thrill my peaceful heart.
And is it true there be yet one,
   Ah, e'en myself can worthy be,
While Virtue's grace all others shun,
   That Cupid so hath favoured me.

'Twere happiness indeed to think
   That my poor love sufficient be,
And that with mine thy soul might link,
   'Twere simple bliss indeed for me.
Thy sylphic strains of love so clear
   Are falling softly o'er my heart ;
Too real, too true, for me I fear,
   So good and guileless as thou art.

I lie beside the gentle stream,
    And there my burdened heart reveal;
Of thee, the object of my theme
    I sing, till death my lips may seal.
Then partly hushed, the stream sings on,
    Its sweetest music stealing o'er,
Lamenting for the spirit gone,
    Yet singing for its love the more.

Its course I take—through gorges roam
    'Neath scars and towering cliffs above,
That seem to pierce the mighty dome,
    And there for thee proclaim my love.
The dashing torrent as it flows
    Descending with the echo clear,
Fills all the valley as it goes
    With sounds of love, as rich as dear.

Love seems to rest upon thy brow,
    A brilliant and a beacon there.
Defying aught, as ever, now,
    To dim or veil its lustre fair.
By giving crystals from thy store,
    The jewelled casket of thy mind,
Thou wilt enrich thyself the more
    And garlands of such gems wilt find.

The melting eyes and gentle smile
   Betray thine heart, thy soul and all ;
Or longer let me dream awhile
   Ere I from airy towers fall.
Ah ! no, dear love, the precious gift
   Is real, all shadows I dismiss :
No veil of doubt I have to lift
   The truth is felt—a loving kiss.

LARMA.

—

Bright the night across the moorland
In the moonlight clear and balmy,
Gentle shadows, scarcely marking
Bush or bramble, stone or hedgerow.
Far-off hills and pretty meadows
Met the eye in distant landscape,
When 'twas lifted from the heather.

Yet the night was cold and lonely
As sweet Larma trod the pathway;
She the dark-eyed maiden, Larma,
Trending onward to the trysting
Of her lover, strong-armed Cosmo:
Far renowned in battle frenzy
For a cool and wise withholding
Of a sword stroke fierce and swinging,
Flashing down on brazen helmet.
He of strong and Gothic beauty
Yet of smooth and winning lip-grace,
So beguiled the pretty Larma
She would meet him where directed.

Why it was her brother Oscar
Liked not Cosmo, knew not Larma.
Loved she Oscar much, yet softly,
Firmly held she tender longing
For her heart's love, Cosmo.   Many
Were the times, surmising Cosmo
Wooed her, that he cautioned Larma
While predicting mischief waiting
On the heels of bonded courtship ;
Little heeded such words spoken
Ever, Love enthroned before them.

Hence her eager steps now speeding
To the hill beside the pine copse,
Not so far from her own dwelling
That she feared the night walk over
Trivial stretch of moorland peaceful.

Ere she left more sheltered footpaths
She had heard the night-gale cheering,
And it made her spirit quicken
To the notes, and burst she lowly
Into mellow song.   Now, hark ye—
" Mighty Spirit tell me truly,
As a maiden, tell me duly
Who my love, and what intending,
What of good or ill impending.

Him I love, oh, what his name is ;
If he love me, what his fame is.
Mighty Spirit, tell me surely,
Wedded life, should love be purely,
Will it mine be ?   Will it mine be ?
Sounds I hear now shall the sign be."

Larma ceased.   Expectant, merry,
With her thought of what would answer
In the lonely night air.   Silence,
All that echoed back suppressed her.
Nearing now the place appointed,
Forcing what of cheer still hovered
O'er her disappointment, fearing
Lest her lover were not come yet,
Suddenly she heard the sword's clash
Loudly ringing through the calmness
Of the quiet night, and, shrieking
Wildly, " Cosmo," heard for answer
Words like, " Ruthless villain, never."
Heeding not the sign appealed for,
Bravely hurried Larma forward.
There her brother Oscar, lifeless
Lay upon the scanty heather ;
Other there was none accounting
For the strife, unless the shadows

H

Presently would move to tender
Mortal witness. Solitary,
Still, an awful terror seized her ;
Fear of something yet to follow ;
What she knew not. Bats were flying
O'er her in their sudden coming,
Sudden disappearing, making
Weird occasion of a moment.

Turning to her brother Oscar,
Kneeling heard she footsteps falling ;
Then a shriek both loud and piercing,
Voiced the night air, " Oscar, Cosmo."
Slowly Cosmo came before her
Like a caitiff fetter burdened.
" Larma, Larma, be not frightened,
Near thee I have been awaiting.
Had he not been brother to thee
Now I would not say I sorrowed.
Quarrelled sore had we, and fighting
Fairly, one was slain ; oh, Larma !
Never wilt thou know how Oscar
Chafed and bearded me concerning
Thee, last words of his declaring,
Thou should'st ne'er be mine." " I heard it,"
Then she cried, " And thou hast murdered
Oscar." " Nay, my pretty sweetheart,

Nay it is not so.   For fearing
I, for what I know not, sweetheart,
Blessed might be in holy wedlock
With my Larma, he in malice
Unexplained would here have slain me
To prevent it."   " He had reason,"
Larma said, " Oh, surely something
Had my brother for his action.
Oscar, tell me, oh, my Oscar."
" Larma, wilt forswear then coldly
All thy loving trust and promise
At first sight of trouble ? "   " Oscar,"
Was her answer, " Can I, should I
Love the man who slew my brother ?
Cosmo, Cosmo, thou forsworn art,
Slaying Oscar, part of Larma ;
She is wounded, may be dying
Thy renown is gone for ever.
'Mongst thy comrades for thy wisdom
And command of mercy dealing
Forth the grace stroke.   Did I hear him
Call thee ruthless ?   Yea, then truly
Heaven shows me what thy fame is ;
Yet, oh, Cosmo, once I loved thee.
Cosmo, O my heart is breaking."
" Come, dear Larma ; come, despair not.
Come to me, my Larma, fear not."

"Touch me not, Oh, touch me never,"
Larma cried, "O, Oscar, Oscar."
Fell she now beside her brother.
Cosmo would have raised her, dared he ;
Coming nearer so attempting ;
But her brother as by spasm
Seemed to try to clutch his dagger.
Larma read the nervous movement
In an instant as intended
For herself, and, as a falcon
Falls upon its prey, she seized it,
Dashed it into Cosmo's heart-core,
Then withdrawing quickly thrust it
In her own fair bosom.   Slowly
Sank she o'er her brother's body
Saying, " Never, Oscar, never.
I will keep thy word, my brother."
Through the trees a wind now sighing
Breathed a requiem sad and mournful,
And the moon's light seemed near waning
By a cloud's dark mantle veiling ;
Wide the shamed retiring landscape.
Ages after 'twas related,
Shades among the trees were hovering,
And that sounds of metal clanging
Heard were 'midst the weirder calling
Of sweet Larma's answer, " Never."

ADIEU TO THE NEIGHBOURHOOD OF THE UPPER THAMES.

—

Adieu, ye pleasant meads,
  Ye scented pastures fair ;
Adieu, ye brown-topped reeds
  And all ye waters bear.
Sweet was the time and joy
  Beside thy fragrance spent ;
Sweet, too, thy blushes coy
  First in the morning lent.

Adieu, ye flowing brooks,
  Ye rippling, sparkling waves,
Caw on, ye sable rooks,
  Sound fill thine elmic naves.
I go, to con no more
  In sylvan Nature's tome,
Its rosy pages o'er,
  Nor midst its scenes to roam.

Adieu, oh, radiant sheen
   Ye pretty flowers wild
On high, ye larks, careen,
   For me ye have beguiled.
I leave fair gales to thee
   Th' enchantment of the woods,
Sing on, sing yet thy glee
   When others don their hoods.

Adieu, my simple bark,
   As trim as trim can be.
Ye swans with saffron arc
   As pure as snow to see.
Sail on and breast the stream,
   With pride no travesty,
Sail full with feathered beam
   In silent majesty.

Adieu, ye nooks and bowers,
   Sunlit, but shadow cool,
Happily pass the hours
   Where trees o'er-branch a pool.
Ye haunts of joy I leave,
   Thy scenes in rapture shared,
My hope and trust I weave
   To come again if spared.

BOAT SONG.

—

Floating gaily down the stream
  Passing bank and meadow sweet,
Filled the air with sunny gleam
  Dancing as with fairy feet.
     And I see the while I lie,
     Fast the world e'er gliding by.

Fair above and bright below
  Dazzling sheen around I see,
Strong in light and charming glow,
  Glad of shade by leafy tree.
     And I see the while I lie,
     Fast the world e'er passes by.

Cool and peaceful haunts I pass,
  'Neath the willow's pendant branch,
Pictured round the silvered glass
  Wherein Nature seems to blanch.
     And I see the while I lie,
     Fast the world e'er gliding by.

Happy, young, and full of life,
   Pleasant are the days and free,
Should I dream of age and strife
   Whilst a care ne'er comes to me ?
      And I see the while I lie,
      Fast the world e'er passes by.

Quickly row thee, brother, row,
   Shadows lengthen o'er the land,
Light is waning, sinking low,
   Yet the going is more grand.
      And I see the while I lie,
      Fast the world e'er gliding by.

Mark the sparkling golden light
   Flecking with its own rich brown
All the grain in fielded might
   Reaching to the distant down.
      And I see the while I lie,
      Fast the world e'er passes by.

Gone the glory, gone the day,
   Light of life is now no more ;
Linger all things as they may,
   Wearied all is o'er and o'er.
      And I see the while I lie,
      Fast the world e'er gliding by.

Comes the night of life, of day,
  Comes a darkness, and a fear,
Time when man must hie away,
  When it darker shall appear.
      And I see the while I lie,
      Fast the world e'er passes by.

Care once scorned when feeling strong,
  Bound in youth and manhood gone
Comes with all its terrors long ;
  Gone the dream, I rested on.
      And I see the while I lie,
      Fast the world e'er gliding by.

Brother, row, a beacon far
  There in thickest darkness see,
Like the light of Heaven's star,
  It must Life's fair harbour be.
      And I see the while I lie,
      Fast the world e'er passes by.

HISTORY :

AN ODE.

—

Hail ! gaunt recorder of the past !
Hail thou, Oh, History ! nor cast
Aside thine awful pen to lull
Us in oblivion, for we cull
    The gay and dread
    Of times now dead,
From yellow pages of thy work,
And many tales of goodness lurk
Therein, by which to welcome thee,
Of nobleness and chivalry.

Roll on, oh, History ! Time shall bring,
What to relate, and what to sing,
And what to mourn for, what to laud.
Times of disease and of the sword ;
Such things that e'en to think of fill with awe,
And yet but what some near departed saw.

Oh ! raise thy harp and voice once more,
And tell thy story as of yore,
Of battles and heroic deeds,
Of armoured knights and fiery steeds ;
    And tell again
      In sorrow then,
    With melancholy song
    Of old domestic wrong,
Where ended the invidious strife
T' engage the fell assassin's knife.

    Strike, oh, minstrel hoary ;
    Strike thy harp of glory !
And ere the light of setting sun
May leave us, let a field be won,
A kingdom lost, its sovereign slain ;
And chant his lady's grief and pain ;
For 'tis an item in the era of the world ;
A scroll for yet another age to see unfurled.

Oh ! but for thee, historic reed !
    An Egypt had been barren now
Alike of interest as of deed,
    And darkness had oppressed the brow.
Thy monuments its legends bear
    Though oft but stones for wandering o'er

And broken for a merchant's store,
So all who wish a chip may share :
But, oh ! a touch of thine,
They reign majestic in their lore,
Inscribed with line and line
They sacred are for evermore.

A staff to living man
Is History's giant span ;
Helping through the ages
Weary travelled sages.
It guides a state when nearly blind
The path of policy to find ;
For often is the gulf of doubt
Bridged over by a page from out
Good olden History ; for such
Has been its universal touch
That scarce an action in the present time,
But what has been before. And like a chime
The ringers send from yonder tower
In the autumnal twilight hour
Will be repeated yet again,
Again, again, and yet again.

Are sweet Arcadian stories dead ?
The meads where Chloe's lambs were fed
All passed away ?
And classic lay

Of Helen, Hector, Dido, Æneas gone?
No chained barbarian slave to look upon?
  Ah! time will make its slaves,
  Its beauties and its braves;
Will give a sweet romance to passing scenes,
And throw a virtue o'er the royal queans.
  And adumbrations fine
  Surrounding Proserpine
  Will gorgeous be and gay
  In sumptuous array,
As art and fancy can then paint them,
And retrospective views acquaint them.

Yea, at thy fane, oh, History!
  Thy votaries shall kneel,
Their worship shall be mystery,
  Emotion, what they feel
    The rather than they show;
    And incense thought.
  Then shall thy spirit flow,
    The solace sought,
All from thy shrine, as to instil
  A gratitude and awe;
Ennobled frames shall feel the thrill
  Of thine enduring law.

Historic melody, flow on, nor stay
   The echoing music of the sea volute,
Where in the wind and rippling waters play,
    Yet sings no more and thy sweet voice be mute
        Oh ! strike its lyre !
      Ye mellow winds ! ye waters soft !
       And raise the fire
     And soul of History aloft.

THE BETROTHAL.

—

There they stood by the murmuring river,
    As it sparkled along by their feet,
While the arrow of love left its quiver
    To be sheathed in a heart ever sweet.
Neither dreamed of a care nor a sorrow,
    Nor presaged an exception to peace,
It was love both to-day and to-morrow
    And a love that the next would increase.

There beside them the stream still was flowing
    O'er the stones ever onward it rolled,
Never upward reflection bestowing
    On the words there so often heard told.
Ever strong while a Spring wind was sighing,
    Ever full for a bright summer's rain,
Yet the winter, less sunshine supplying,
    By its coldness its force would restrain.

Was the Summer or Winter prevailing ?
    O, thou silvery rivulet tell,
O, what vessel of life was there sailing
    O'er the main of that beautiful dell ?
It was neither.   'Twas Autumn all charming,
    And a bark smoothly gliding in peace
On a sea with no prospect alarming,
    Yet with anchor no power could release.

LOVE'S CLOUD.

Oh, who can tell what sun shall rise
   On this my night of woe,
When clouds so dark float o'er the skies
   And leave no light below,
Canst pierce the depth of shadow there
   The veil of sorrow here,
And show a gleam of radiance fair
   To brighten or to cheer ?

How gently love will hold its grief,
   In silent pain will mourn ;
E'en shrink from what would give relief
   And confidence e'er scorn.
So strong that years will scarcely melt
   The sweetness of its bonds ;
Caressed as though its kiss was felt,
   As though its love responds.

I

Kind words may soften or e'en charm
    Away the sharper pain,
But love to love can bring no balm
    To heal a broken strain.
Yet as the cloud may break and leave
    A brilliance clear to view,
So will the rain of tears retrieve
    The calm that once it knew.

AN AWAKENING.

—

When thought comes crowding quickly o'er
  And fickle senses are bewildered
Leave me to wander by the shore,
  To scan the sea like metal silvered.
The soothing distance soon becalms,
  Flickering seams and lights absorbing,
Like spots of red on canvas charms,
  Or echoes loud of night birds warbling.

The wood, the field, the fen or moor
  Might lead me far, such thoughts distracting,
The will-o'-the-wisp to death allure
  'Twould fascinate, the while attracting,
I would the one thought think well out,
  Forge it and batter it, approving,
Till shapely wrought, 'twas fit about
  The world to go for ever moving.

This to a valley once led me,
   Woody and bright, yet so lone,
Bright in the sunshine all golden,
   Drear when the sun-orb was prone,
Velvety soft was the carpet
   Nature had strewn o'er the glade
Grasses and daisies all bowing
   Gently, as progress I made.

Dwelling on themes e'er so lightly,
   'Tent on unravelling one,
How yet and why the Almighty
   Stayed not fell sickness its run.
Seeing how Nature could gladden
   Man with its beauty and form,
Why the allowance to sadden
   Animal grandeur by storm?

Humbly I granted solution ;
   Demonstrate ; no, not at all.
Was it by weird evolution
   Victims to plague-sores might fall ?
Dubiously pondering slowly
   Fell there a waft of a sigh,
Consciousness woke to a lowly
   Weeping and wailing close nigh.

Slender reeds breaking or bending,
   Stately the branch that is shed,
Cankered disease ever blending
   Glories of life with the dead.
Ambient the landscape and smiling
   Sweetly o'erburdened the air;
Gracious and pleasant the whiling
   Twilight away where so fair.

Young was the maid I discovered
   Lying the ground full along,
Wild was her hair and uncovered,
   Grief to despairing was strong ;
Figure well-moulded and seeming
   Goodly of stature was she
Why was the madness so teeming ?
   'Twas to console her and see.

Still pretty hands, pretty fingers,
   Palm-pressed her face on the ground,
Springs there a brook as she lingers,
   Welling from eyelids yet bound.
Cheer thee, young lady, come cheer thee,'
   Tell me if aught can be done.
Let me uplift thee, nor fear me,
   Do not my offices shun.

'Tis so I seem to see her
Now before mine eyes,
'Tis so I seem to see her,
Slowly, slowly rise.
Turning her face then towards me quite gently,
Stood I aghast at the awful disclosure,
Fixedly gazing observed I intently,
Causes that marred and disturbed my composure.

Dark was the cavernous eye,
Sallow the face and thin,
Scarred from her forehead full high,
Deeply to mouth and chin.
There vile disease had done well,
Cancelling beauty lines,
Casting all o'er her a spell,
Misery, death enshrines.

Looking at me she replied,
" Thou too then loathest me,"
Go ye then, why dost thou bide,
Aid is not asked of thee.
One e'en professed to adore,
Ground that I walked upon,
Ribbons or gloves that I wore,
Such 'twas I trusted on.

" Tokens of love and fair words
    Had I then breathed to me,
Sweet as the songs of the birds,
    Soft as their cooings be.
Gems, too, of ruby and pearl
    Clustered with brilliants were,
Kissed he the finger or curl,
    Each had his jealous care.

" Kissed he this mouth and this face,
    Kissed he mine eyes and brow,
Oh, that pale Death would efface
    Lingering memories now.
'Beautiful,' often he said,
    Echoed the mirror so,
Soon e'en we were to be wed—
    Now 'twill be never so.

" Yes, he has seen me and flown,
    Flying my touch as 'twere ;
Oh, that he erst could have known,
    There was no mark elsewhere.
Faithless, yet censure I not,
    But that I loved him so,
More 'tis a pity for what,
    Lost he of love I know."

'Twas then I tried to cheer her,
  Trouble to disarm,
When standing there so near her
  Kindness lent its charm,
Gently her hand therefore taking,
  Telling her God never thought of one's beauty,
Still though so sadly awaking,
  'Twould from the world yet uplift her to duty.

Comes a something we wished long ago
  Or an answer we did not expect,
At a time perhaps burdened with woe,
  Or a moment by pleasure bedecked.
Knew I now why disease had its sway
  O'er the casement of flesh and of bone,
Fiercely burning the crucible's clay,
  Hardly leaving the jewel alone.

For the fire that so burneth what thought?
  For the clay that contains it what care?
'Tis the soul's golden gem that is sought,
  But the way of refining it ne'er.
'Tis a part of our God and divine;
  Of a Spirit, an Angel the germ,
But the casket, however so fine;
  May consumed be by fire or the worm.

'Twas a teaching 'gainst doubt of a cause,
  And possession it took of my heart ;
Then resolved I for ever to pause
  Ere the faith in a theme might depart.
And the quiet and peace that befell
  O'er my mind as I homeward returned,
Like the hush of the trees in the dell
  Was the lullaby nature had earned.

DISCOVERY OF EARTHLY LOVE.

—

Oh ! hide, oh ! hide, my darling,
   Hide thy blushes on my breast,
And I will sooth thee, sweet one,
   Whilst our thrilling hearts are pressed.
Thine eyes bespeak thy feeling,
   Scarcely need I tell thee mine,
Oh ! darling, I embrace thee,
   Ever, ever am I thine.

Oh ! do not answer, dearest,
   Know I well what thou wouldst say,
Thy swelling bosom speaks, love,
   Of thy secret flown away.
Look up to me, mine own one,
   Linger here, devoted frame,
Thy soul will ever stay, love,
   Mine is bounden with its name.

This ecstacy of love, dear,
    Filled with happy dreams for aye,
Lulls time in balmy sleep, love,
    Moments passing as they may ;
But yet a little longer
    Blending our affection here,
And we will fly together
    To uniting bowers, dear.

IN SEARCH OF HEAVENLY LOVE.

—

Let us fly far away,
  Let us seek far above,
Through the night, through the day,
  Till we find us pure love;
Left the false is behind,
  We have nought now not true,
What relief to the mind,
  World of evil adieu!

'Tis a bird—a white dove,
  That we follow so fleet,
With no guile in its love,
  Nor treads evil its feet.
As in innocence soars
  Yonder bird in the air,
O'er our being it pours
  Its own virtue so rare.

But the essaying wings
  Sadly tire as they wend,
Love it shews with its springs,
  Then it leaves to descend ;
Now we find Love's domains,
  And pure realms so profound,
Songs of love and sweet strains
  Are re-echoing round.

All are good where it dwells,
  All return it, and love
Him above from Whom swells
  The refulgence of love ;
All around it imbues
  With its mystical chord,
Songs of praise are its dues,
  'Tis the Lamb is its Lord.

THE PRINCE IMPERIAL.

IN MEMORIAM.

June 1, 1879.

—

Oh, Prince! thy destiny hath sought and found
  Thee by a savage hand, nor led, nor taught
By human skill. And e'en hard by the sound
  Of comrade's bugle, that would have proudly
      wrought
Thy saving from the fated agent, if the Power
  On High had so directed ; but for some
Great good that Power withheld direction. Hour
  Of dearth unto thy mother, it shall come
Hereafter to be shewn that wisdom swayed
  The fatal brand. Not lost, but as a star
Eclipsed. Thine early death surprised, dismayed
  An island empire, which although afar
Esteemed thee ; for endeared to it by choice
  Of exile, thou, companion of its arms,
Offeredst thy sword in nobly valiant voice ;

Away didst go amidst the dread alarms
Of Kaffir prowess to their land, for sake
Of progress and enlightenment, to dare
Their cunning and their clime, and so to break
And tame the savage humour. It was there
Like many others thou hast fallen, then
Thy part was done—thy mission ended. Man
Thou would'st have civilised. Wast martyred when
Thou hadst intent to offer love. What ban
Is held o'er that dark race ? The curse of old.
Then let his favoured brother teach the way
To find new grace. Then to the Shepherd's fold
Shall come blest thousands multiplied each day.
Beloved Prince we mourn thee with the heart
Of friendship ; for thy parent's sake we mourn,
They having rested on our shores in part
A lifetime. Thine Imperial sire was borne
Away for ever, e'en for ever, here
Whilst sojourning. And thou Prince would'st
    have raised
His shield, and shaken off the fallen tear ;
Have earned the laurel, and for deeds been
    praised,
Hadst not thy dauntless heart been laid so low
Thus soon. Ah ! now Napoleon's spirit sleeps.
It came, it went, as shadows come and go,
But as the legend ends, a nation weeps.

Bereaved, dejected, sorrowing lady ! calm
    Thy soul with knowledge of a greater throne
Than aught terrestrial gives. The transient charm
    Of sovereignty is as the minor tone
Of evening to the thunders of a grand
    Celestial glory.   He, thy son, hath gained
A mansion in the higher places ; land
    Alike of chivalry and good attained,
From which he sees thee weeping, weeping yet,
    Yea, even in thy chamber. Oh ! how lone
Thy heart is ! how void ! the sun hath set
    To thee, the night hath come to find thee prone
In tears.   Yet shalt thou find a comfort there ;
    Where once was youthful joy and buoyant life,
Filled with glad dreams of future, gilded fair,
    Ere realising its awakening strife.
Yearns thy sad heart to be with him, thy son ?
    Deem the hour chosen wise, it bringeth peace,
Assuages trouble, and beguiles the run
    Of moments, whilst awaiting that release
We may not hasten.   Heaven ! oh, lift the veil
    Of grief and comfort her.
                              Hold, foeman, hold
Thy voice in silence, doff the tempered mail
    Of enmity—thy feud for aye is told.
Dead are the hopes and dreams maternal. Dead
    The tongue of envy ; yet will live a sense

And feeling as of paths the angels tread,
   And from the sphere of spirits hieing thence
To life eternal, where shall those we knew
   Ere long be met, and as of greeting there,
As glides another shade within their view,
   Which, guided, soars unto their jealous care.

BERNARD AND SYLVIA.

A DUET.

—

BERNARD—

    I come to claim thee now, my love,
      Though years have passed away
    Since words so fair of promised trust
      Were breathed upon a day.
    These haunts recall the pleasures sweet,
      That all too swiftly ended.

TOGETHER—

BERNARD { And now again } those { do } meet
SYLVIA { Though never } hearts { may }
      more

    Which long ago were blended.
      The silvery sheen
      A beauteous scene,
    And still with deepening shadows
      All casting clear
      A quaintly drear
    Enchantment o'er the meadows.

BERNARD—

    The moon half full, o'er yonder pine,
      And brilliant e'en as now,
    With stars by thousands that now shine

TOGETHER—

    Bore witness of our vow.

SYLVIA—

    Ah! yes, and oft this tranquil spot
      My steps have wandered o'er,
    In memory sweet of loving things
      Too lightly told before.
    For dreams have shown thee dwelling not
      On scenes of old so charming,

TOGETHER—

SILVIA   { But, for the new, old love } forgot,
BERNARD   { No, no, my love was ne'er }

    All
    No } constancy disarming.

      In foreign lands

      Your
      Our } hearts and hands

    Beguiled by
    Though under } beauty's power,

      And led to roam

      Forget { old / not } home

   { As flies to change their flower ;
   { For happiest is its bower.

So leave me then to weep and ⎫ pine
The moon half full o'er yonder ⎭

And sorrowing ⎫ as now,
And brilliant e'en ⎭

Though ⎫ stars by thousands ⎰ which yet ⎱ shine
With   ⎭   ⎱ that now ⎰

Bore witness of our vow.

BERNARD—

That such, thy fancies, love, are false
  Thine own dear heart shall tell,
As dreams are of another world
  Love contradicts the spell.
Awake we have things as they are,
  In sleep it is but dreaming :
Asleep no love, no life, no star ;
  Awake we have the seeming.

TOGETHER—

      Possess we all
      And faith withal.
  Then full our heart's sweet measure.

BERNARD ⎰ Dear love be mine.
 SYLVIA ⎱ And am I thine ?

      And ⎫ I am thine
      Yes ⎭

  For ever ⎰ oh, what ⎱ pleasure.
           ⎱ if your ⎰

With clinging love our hearts entwine,
  E'er trusting each as now,
Remembering how the stars that shine
  Bore witness of our vow.

A HYMN.

—

Take thou, O beauteous Light, my will,
  My thought, my life, my all ;
As shadows lifted o'er the hill
  Are gathered up from fall.
Far back in years my spirit soared
  On high, as thine possessed ;
As well, O now accept, restored
  My body still caressed.

Let me be thine at moment's call
  If I on earth remain,
And let me do what may befall ;
  Yet all of thine ordain.
Oh, what to me the powers borne
  Of mind, or body whole ;
Already I of part am shorn,
  And that my very soul.

Now I have seen thee I am thine ;
　Me take or leave me here ;
I all the world fore'er resign,
　But thou, O Light, be near.
For all is dark without thy gleam,
　Which strengthens all my frame ;
Withdraw it not, O thou Supreme,
　Lest I should lose my aim.

A HYMN.

Oh! loved Creator we come nearer,
   Though slowly, surely, unto Thee,
And yet 'tis sweeter, and e'en dearer,
   All knowing what the end will be.
The way we journey e'er gets lighter
   Becomes the smoother, better known,
Becomes yet grander, and yet brighter
   As our glad footsteps near Thy throne.

Most Holy, Great and Mighty! singing,
   Thy glory praising every voice,
We come to Thee our offerings bringing,
   Our heart's while worshipping rejoice.
With loud Hosannas now vibrating
   Through space and distant regions fair,
Our souls to Thee all consecrating
   To meet the Saviour all prepare.

Behold the Lamb approaches slowly,
　　With searching glance on us around,
Then claims us all.   Ah! yet so lowly,
　　Sorrowing that no more are found.
Great King of Kings, triumphant glory
　　Is Thine, O Lord, for evermore ;
Dear Jesus' own appear before Thee,
　　To be beloved, to love restore.

A HYMN.

Our hearts are full of praise,
  Almighty God, of thee,
And this our song we raise,
  In swelling harmony.
Endow, O Lord, with grace
  Our hallelujahs bold,
Resounding through the space
  Of these thy transepts old.

Our gladsome voices search
  The canopies of gold,
And fill thy towering church
  With music yet untold.
We know no grateful sound
  Can reach thee up on high,
But thou art here around,
  For ever, ever nigh.

Yet 'tis but passing wind,
   A sound, nor loud, nor clear,
Unworthy of the kind
   Creator's love and ear,
For sending us His Son
   Far from the realms above,
He then a triumph won,
   And taught us all to love.

A HYMN.

—

Lord ! all guilty, wretched I,
  Weeping, sad and weary, lone,
Come to claim of thee on high
  Part of thy great mercy shown.
Brethren, who are in thy grace
  Tell me of thy loving care,
And that thou hast turned thy face
  Never from a sinner's prayer.

Humbly I before thee throw
  All of self and worldly thought
That e'er cast me to and fro,
  Gaining never what I sought.
See I now the light around
  Of the Spirit's holy hand ;
Hark ! the blessing—joyous sound,
  Comes to me by thy command.

Praise, my God.   Oh, praise to thee,
   Ever, ever will I sing ;
Chorus, hymns and holy glee,
   All with sweetest music bring.
And great hallelujahs strong
   Shall our voices gladly raise,
While our souls to thee belong,
   Then for ever will we praise.

AGNES; OR, THE HILLY PATH.

A ROMANCE OF FIFTY YEARS AGO.

—

ARGUMENT.

PART I.—Young Edmund Dalreigh surprises and shocks his tutor, Albert, by asking if he might love his sister, Agnes. He is advised to go abroad to get more worldly experience, when Edmund assures his tutor, seeing the old man is hurt, that he only loves Agnes as a brother. Albert's son comes from his adopted home in France and attempts to beguile Edmund into going abroad by gay visions of life. Albert attempts to crush these vicious ideas.

PART II.—Albert acts as organist, and is discovered in Chapel. Edmund and Herbert become great friends. Sir Hugh Dalreigh discovered, seated with Agnes, Sybil and Edmund, by Albert, who tells him that his son, Herbert has brought news of his sister's death, and his own accession to an estate. Music and singing. Herbert falls in love with Sybil.

PART III.—At an assembly in the hall, **Sir Hugh**
asks how Herbert came to live in
France. Albert tells him the tale how
his daughter was lost. Sir Hugh, in
turn, tells him a story how he found
a little girl. **Discovery of Agnes.**
Edmund then loves Agnes, **and**
Herbert Sybil. After going abroad,
Albert comes to live near them.

AGNES ; OR, THE HILLY PATH.

—

" Behold the morn, and view the scene around,
'Tis as the early mist is swept before
The genial warmth of heaven's glowing fire,
The mist of ignorance in early life
Is swept before the rays of knowledge vast,
And with the heat of charmed enlightenment
Awakes the opening landscape, whilst we gaze
And ponder o'er fresh beauties, not till now
Unfolded to our senses.   Wafted sounds
Now play about the ear a gambol gay,
Proclaimed as music sweet. Surprised and pleased,
Awhile 'tis lost, but onward wending, back
Returns in charming echoes : oh ! how great,
How mighty is the hand in harmony,
Creating atoms, which perchance may form,
By combination of their elements,

The simple buttercup, or canopied
Immensity of Nature's dome above ;
Each glorifies by grandeur !"

                       Thus he spoke,
Young Edmund's tutor Albert, who yet stood
As though still pouring forth his inmost soul
In silent veneration, but who now
Turned round to Edmund, saying, anxiously,
" Come, Edmund, thou art silent, thou art sad,
Thy sadness overwhelms thy tongue, absorbs
Thy thought, come tell me why, that I may cheer
Thee."

    " Nay," then Edmund answered, " If I speak
Of what enchains my tongue, thou wilt not cheer,
But chide ; I have no heart, no mind for scenes
Which make thee thankful, Albert.   Thoughts will
    come,
That half desired, yet half rejected, seem
To balance in the scale of moral worth,
Or good or sinful, either battling each,
Which so confuses and absorbs, that speech
Runs renegade ; but now I will enlist
Thine ear : I love my sister Agnes much
As lover loves, and as a brother should—
'Tis this that cramps my brain in agony
And holds the power of sense in useless pain,
Yet working war amidst the awful din

Of mobbing thoughts.   Now Albert, think,
Imagine to thyself a hell-bound troop
Of fiendish sprites all tumbling, tramping o'er
The foil stretched cavern of an anxious mind,
Metallic cymbals clanging, dashing on
With headlong rout and noise, and ceasing not
'Tis there my thoughts shall be to find the way
The which to follow.   Do I by my love
Hazard the fairer telling of our honour
Think ye ? or whether by a deeper love
Than youthful brothers show, there may not be
Together yoked a sister's love with mine,
So adding happiness to this uncouth
Unhappy world ? "

                " Now stay, now stay, no more,"
Said Albert.   " I have waited long to hear
Thy meaning, and am grieved to hear thee speak
Such wayward virtue.   Have I toiled to find
Thee thus ?   But nay, I cannot think it so—
That thou thyself would'st rather lie beneath
The grassy mound of death, experience
Bespeaks my inward soul, but loving her
The more than sister grieves me, for 'tis like
The phantom arch that spans the semi-world
Of thy existence, and 'neath which there glooms
A darksome cloud, although it soon must pass
Away—hard pressed by zephyr's from a source

Of goodly prayer and grace—or it will drown
Thee in deep floods of shame. So list awhile
And thou shalt hear now from these aging lips,
The love I bear thee, for I love to walk
With thee at dawn, to sit at morning meal,
To study and to aid thee at thy work
The while the sun is rising as in flight,
To dine with thee and talk with thee till eve,
To play, to sing, to sup with thee, when night
Doth part us until morn, and then I greet
Thee with an earnest love, and strong the more
For being parted for a space. But now
I see that we must part, for thou awhile
Shouldst go ; shouldst journey Europe's modern
  stage.
My son, I tell thee go to France, to Spain,
And Learning's centre, Germany, and then
To much sought Italy, an empire once,
Anon a wreck ; the doom of all things—
And so see many countries, changing oft,
And so shall change thy love. I pray thee go,
Although my hairs may whiten by my grief."

" Well, be it, kindly Albert, as thou wilt,
My sister Agnes hath but brother's love;
But see now here she comes, and greeting us
Though with a stranger, Albert, knowest him ? "

Now Albert's visage saddened as he said :
"Ay, ay, it is my son, what does he here,
Or has he drone-like come to feed upon
And waste the sweetness of our laboured store ?
Oh! heed him not, or he with foreign scenes
Will charm thee to the slough of gaiety."

But Agnes with her now brought Herbert near,
And kindly were the greetings and sincere,
Then Agnes with her brother walked apart,
And wandered through the then all-welcome
        shades
Of bark-peeled sycamore and linden trees,
And treading lightly o'er the mossy grass,
Their hearts rejoiced. Sweet notes and chirping
        songs,
Which now poured forth from many feathered
        throats,
Inflate the welkin, and with fulsome sounds
Nigh strained it. Clinging each to each they
        strolled.
And Agnes lifted up her eyes to him,
Then whispered, pointing to the cloudless sky,
" Yet thinkest thou 'tis happier there ? "

                              "Oh, bliss !
Unfathomable bliss ! when earth is heaven,
To human hearts, oh, what must heaven be ! "

He thought, and said, " Dear Agnes, ere thou
    hadst seen
Yon lily there, come, didst thou not proclaim
The other ' best ? '   Consider then the world
A lily fair, but one to be surpassed
By that which opes profoundly grand above."

" Oh, why are we not always happy here,
Would not the spirit of the world be high ?
The lighter for exemption from all harm ;
While goodness reigning and dispensing good,
Would raise the ether of the soul near Heaven
Itself.   We then might bid good-night to sin,
And on the morrow be in paradise,"
She said ; and he, " Dear Agnes, this is hope,
A goodly mansion built on happiness,
But towering to an over-clouded point
Is lost to view 'cept to itself, and so
When happy here we soar, as does the lark,
In aspiration to the distant sky,
Conceiving there to gain a happier sphere,
Until we prove its very vanity
A myth, and turn to Earth, as all things must,
To nestle on its shores, our only rest.
Are there not dreams by day as well as night ?
Beware the pool the while the brain is weak
And only wise in sleep ; for weaker then,

'Tis madly prone to follow any wisp
That lights its way to self-destruction.   Sleep
By day, alike by night, reveals a path
All fairy-trod, to richer life that when
Awake one dares not follow ; for 'tis then
The foolish mind, made conscious, sadly views
The folly that it thought so wise in deep
But transient slumber.   We are played with thus,
Hard beaten by the battledore of time ;
But as I may not overcast thy day
Together we will sing that praiseful song
Good Albert sang one eve, some days ago."
And they in sweetest melody began
Their song :

    'Tis when the spirit of the mind
      Is soothed by Virtue's ways,
    The soul of man is raised on high
      In ecstacy of praise.
    When calm and still the surging brain,
      Unconsciously we sing,
    Our wandering steps to wonders lead
      With fancy on the wing.

    No burden has the grateful heart
      In realms of airy peace,
    For dwelling there it gains a rest
      Beyond desired increase.

So give us such contented life
    As live the forest trees
Whose boughs the grander, nobler show,
    When ruffled by the breeze.

What joy to hearts o'ercharged with love
    Would such existence be,
Where all through fairy visions pass
    And their Elysium see ;
Yet turn to earth, green clad anew,
    Though lowly be the theme,
We there may make a heaven, our own,
    Far truer than a dream.

So blending harmony of thought
With all the music of their voices sweet,
Enraptured from the richly perfumed grove,
Th' emerged to saunter o'er the open glade,
Where soon they met good Albert with his son,
But Agnes then stole quietly away.

The heart may happy be the term it mourns,
Consoled by transient gleams of future rest ;
An old man's wearied mind receives a balm
To sooth his sorrows and to comfort age.
So Albert told how he was called to France,
To mourn his widowed sister, now no more,
But still to take all that she left behind,

Thus leaving him in affluence and in ease.
Would Edmund go with him to Fontenoy,
By travel so to scatter, ruder thoughts,
And clear the brain from incrustations crude ?
" Aye, come," quoth Herbert, " I will show thee
      France,
Its gaiety and pomp which fascinates
Imagination's eye, and teacheth one
To cull vivacity therefrom; its change
Of social forms, which helps us to digest
Its various meats, and filling us with that
Excitement, which then, scarcely e'er leaves room
For melancholy ; noble as ye are
In Britain, lethargy the lion shews
And heaviness the visage of the bull :
Come where the soaring eagle fondly eyes
The glittering sun, and then for change looks down
Upon a royal pompous cavalcade
Below ; come where the fashion is its world
Yet where that fashion wearieth curious minds,
Because the world itself is slow to change
Its shape.   Oh, 'tis a happy life in France."
" Stay, stay, my wandering son and let me ask,
Amongst the many changes France has seen
Is folly changed to reason yet, or aught
But frenzy still ?   Ah ! poor, yet glorious France,
Say what of change has sent enduring peace

Unto its shores, its provinces, its homes ;
Preserved its monarchs, valour, dignity,
Its virtue or nobility ; or saved
Its palaces and villas, prestige, state,
Or has it not laid waste the country side,
Sheathing its sword in blood and wanton strife.
Change it has had.   Change that has bred enough
Dismay to make its neighbours weep for shame,
And mourn the loss of honour in so large
A nation. Say, is this the sought-for change ?
The fascination right to follow ? No,
The temperament of the people differs here,
For he who reigns we love to know doth reign
A virtuous king, and are content with peace ;
But fickle France, beheading him for change,
Would steep the nation deep in ruin, war,
And bloodshed dire, the while its people asked :
What was the newest mode ? Nay, wise will be
The Prince that ever governs it with such
A safety to himself, as lies within
A people's love."

         " The penalty of pain
That e'er attends on pleasure," Herbert said,
" Doth sit but lightly on a Frenchman's brow ;
If fickle 'tis a part and quality
Of life to him ; and sorrow come, he bears

It cheerfully, nor mourns he yet so long
Nor so despairingly, as ye do here.
Though British born a Briton's views I have
Not.   All seems dull and murky here,
As though a cloud o'erhung the island round.
So urge I then its scenery e'er felt
Sufficient to induce the tourist fond
And lover of the grand, to traverse o'er
The narrow straits."

        " I would that all were filled
With somewhat else than pleasure, for it is
The seekers of such trifles e'er, that stock
The world with pain, and find amusement great
I'the agony—the restless gaudy moths
Of human life, that work destruction out."
Thus Albert spoke, and Herbert then returned,
" Well, where is man's superiority ?
Whose life is destitute of ordered plan ;
Where better state ?   Where life inferior ?
The flitting moth that nature favours now,
And then as soon forsakes, is type of man.
The same with things around—a tree is reared
A triumph nature claims, a lusty tree
Full sound and young and in its glorious prime,
Nature nourishes it ; but doth the worm
Not come to undermine its aging life
To break its day of pride and glory too

To leave there but a wrecked and mouldering pile?
'Tis thus is seen a doom eternal, as
Is also seen an ever-checking break
In life, and everywhere that life exists,
And in obscuring mists concealing dire
And unknown destiny, as though to tempt
Us sometimes yet to live in trust and hope,
And yet anon to yield to death's despair.
Is not the man a tree by nature left
When in its prime to rancour and decay,
And to himself a worm of magnitude ?
May we not play a little with that doom ?"

" Prithee, think not so, my son," then Albert said,
" To sober minds the greatest pleasure found,
Might be the calmest recreation sought.
And that same mind superior power gives
To man o'er all the creatures on the globe ;
Nought else hath object other than its will
To please, but man hath the Omnipotent
To glorify by actions here on earth,
And all our pleasures should in some way tend
To such an object.   Nobler minds are given
To man than aught created ; power of thought
And reason.   Peace amongst our kith, our kin,
And nations does not rest upon the will,
But all upon suppression of it.   Things

We have given us subservient to our will,
That we may work and blend them to the use
Of glorifying Him who made the whole—
Us, in His image that we might see and feel
His works.   Wonder and worship !   Is not this
Where lies superiority of man ?
A temple in thyself, debase it not
By thinking thus, my son.   The measure thine
Of peace is rendered unto thee in full
According to thy reverence to One
Who justly claims it."

      " Ah ! " quoth Edmund then
And archly, " Where thine answer, Herbert now ?
Or hath thy father silenced thee ?   For me
Your foreign climes may bask in beauty's sun,
Their landscapes, cities, and their villages
May be the grandest told, but yet there still
Shall be a something dear, a something sweet,
To call me o'er the scenes of native land,
A quiet converse 'tween my spirit lone
And rippling brooks and humble places, where
May happiness be found, before I seek
A path or palace on a foreign soil.
Hast thou no sympathy of soil, my friend ?
Ah ! yes ; thou hast, but somewhat differing."
And presently they parted company.

END OF PART I.

PART II.

Alone our Albert walks, while giving all
The genial atmosphere his truant thoughts,
And mimicking the sounds, the spirit mine,
My faithful Muse thus gave them to mine ear,
" And shall I give my mind to sleep—my frame
To rest, and is the buoyant spirit gone ?
My feebler steps now daily tell me so.
To sleep the hour then like the gorgëd beast !
Oh ! Nature ! let me not give way and lose
The pleasure, that to me is life itself,
Of viewing thee, and listening to the sweet
Melodious sounds of thy dear voice.   What joy
It is to watch the lambkin sporting o'er
The sward, but scarcely heeding for its play
The warning bleats the old ewe sends her young,
Lest it should gambol into harm ; to note
The peaceful cropping of the grass, bedewed
Afresh by recent rain.   Oh ! who would sleep
Who cares for Nature's varied scenes ? Now mark
The shadow of the cloud, as travelling o'er
The fields it lends refreshment to the flocks
And lowing kine, and breaks the scorching rays

From off all things that live and move beneath ;
And is there not a music in the scene ?
And from the tiny things that crawl and fly
Does not the buzzing glow of thankfulness
Arise, assisted by the movement vast
Of countless leaves of vegetation ?   Can
One not deduce a people's music sweet
From ever praiseful song and harmony
Of the created, going up on high
To their Creator ?   For all tones I hear
Around me.   Man but gleaned at harvest time,
When the Almighty gathered in the fruits ;
The scattered notes collected, were then placed
Like all things else subservient to the mind.
Thanks, thanks for power of mind ! And history
      comes
To help our veneration for the gift.
As the wave of the ocean sweeps the shore
And marks its havoc there, so Time—unseen
Particle of eternity—records
In History its potentiality
Indelibly written is the legend quaint,
Stamped in tradition ; as the creviced rock
May show a yawning gulf to stamp its truth.
In all above, beneath, around is power
Dispensed by Him who first created it,
If granted then that all partake of power,

He in creating it, created all.
Thanks, thanks to thee, O God.   But now I near
The village church, which place to all our hearts
Should be most dear."
                And Albert, who had been
The organist for many years, first sought
An old attendant, who as verger served,
Or else was cleaning where no dirt was found,
And then ascending to the organ played
Such varied strains as long experience
Told was harmony,—grandly now and loud,
And then the softly sweet and minor key
Bespoke the praise, and the humility
His heart and soul in turn sent pealing forth.

Here Herbert by his friend accompanied,
In passing near had heard the symphony
And treading lightly 'neath the portal arch,
Now listened to the swelling notes, as through
The spacious edifice they travelled full,
Resounding to the groinëd roof in rich
And powerful measure, piercing nigh their hearts
Unto affecting tears of love to God.
Oh ! list awhile, for now he sings this hymn :—

My God, to thee, my humble voice
  Oh, ever let me raise to thee,
Through tears, oh, let my heart rejoice
  In due and gladdening praise of thee.
For thou hast given me grace to know
  All things were ever made by thee;
So surely I may others show
  What glory should be paid to thee.

No sin, nor heaviness of heart,
  Now burdeneth my song to thee,
Nor envying will I offer part,
  Entirely I belong to thee.
Thy Son took all the sin away,
  Then journeyed far above to thee;
And I behests of His obey,
  To follow on for love of thee.

No darkness do I find around
  The path is light I tread to thee.
Thy promises do e'er resound,
  In every soul not dead to thee.
Oh, help me home when 'tis thy will,
  My heart and soul I give to thee.
My every nerve with hope doth thrill,
  For times when I may live with thee.

And when the cadence ended Albert seemed
To be absorbed in prayer.　The friends went out
With hearts too full to speak till they had walked
Awhile communing with themselves, nor did
They wait for Albert, fearing to disturb
His happy reverie.
　　　　　　Then　Edmund said :
" My sister Agnes and myself have oft
Enjoyed such hours as this ; and then gone home,
Both full of veneration and of love
For all surrounding."
　　　　　　　　" It truly gives
A greater sympathy to one for those
About him, and esteem for things around ;
It shows to one the pettiness of self,
Without the grace Divinity holds out
To us."
　　　　　So Herbert spoke, as though he felt
An inner struggle 'gainst some fresher thought.
And Edmund answered seriously and said :
" I would that thou hadst been the more with him,
Thy father, for he always seemeth good,
Instilling ever good in other minds,
And when rebuking, kind, attracting love,
Yet firmly just, is strong in furthering all
Requiring justice ; so not generous
Unto a fault, but charitable withal.

A friend like this I would not lose for all
The wealth and gaiety, the east or west
Could offer me ; his argument is kind,
His conversation full of energy
To teach ; above the vice of pedantry
He seeks his God to please, and pleasing Him
Is satisfied : I scorn the man who looks
Alone for man to please, though moral may
He be ; if he forget the Deity,
Then rest assured he be forgotten too."

O'er day departed, evening drew the shroud,
And lowering spirits sang their lonely dirge,
Whilst flitting o'er the vales and lands around ;
The darkened air was filled with shadows gaunt,
And weird-like forms appeared athwart the scene :
These things of troubled night were closed from
        view
Of all within the Manor of Dalreigh,
Which now behind a gloomy tuft of trees
Well hid its inner life from all without ;
There dwelt Sir Hugh, who kind, though nobly
        proud,
Esteemed his children as he did himself,
And Edmund, Agnes and his Sybil dear,
All fondly nestled 'neath the spreading wings

Of his paternal care.   There comfort reigned
Throughout the spacious chambers high and low ;
In one they sat, and each made manifest
The gladness, health and due contentment lent.

Then to them Albert with his welcomed son
Came, not as menials, but as honoured guests,
And after many pleasantries had passed,
Friend Albert thus bespoke Sir Hugh :   " From
    France
My son hath brought me hither tidings sad,
My sister is no more—the only one—
Whose husband dying many years ago,
Bequeathed to her of worldly value much,
Which, seemingly, her death has left to me,
And so, my age shall find that goodly rest
That all my life and labour never gave.
Yet not that labour could be sweeter borne
Than in this happy home, where station doffs
Its crest to put thereon the cap of love
And kindness, making labour but an act
Of pleasure, and a semblance but in name.
My service is I think nigh ended here
For neither of your children want me more."

" Speak not to me of service," quoth Sir Hugh,
" That ended long ago, 'tis friendship now,
And glad I am to hear of thy reward

M

And future independence, yet shall grieve
To lose thy company ; for when the sun
Doth set upon an autumn day, although
It seem to e arn a sweet repose, it leaves
A chill behind, for having warmed the life
Of day, we miss its genial disc too soon
Once having felt its warmth."

        " My thanks to thee
For thy esteem, Sir Hugh, may ne'er a cloud
Of discord wafted be atween our hearts,
 Which not too old to feel the glow of warm
And friendly spirit thrilling through our frames,
Have time to dwell in such a blissful peace
As long tried love inherits.   Friendship's fire
In youth is fickle ; take thee heed of words
In warning, O my children ; seldom give
Thy confidence to mortal ; keep thine own,
Yet seeking counsel of the Power above :
For scarce the man that makes a friend,—a gem
When found inestimable, much sought for, yet
Acquired but seldom, for to be a friend,
Or keep a friend, one must nigh perfect be.
But where is he so like his God ?   So let
Experience warn thee of the bitter pangs
Of broken, scattered friendship, whilst thou'rt
  young,
So let it guard thee from its fang-like guile,

Watch long and wait and he will show himself
And yet not to thee, rather for thy ken."

But Herbert's lively nature could not brook
His father's seriousness, so after few
More earnest dialogues between them, asked
Fair Sybil whether she would favour them
By singing something of a joyful air,
At which she timidly but firmly sang :

Sweet the vale where she was dwelling,
 Sweet the meeting in the evening,
 With the loved one near the river,
Where her heart for him was swelling.

Haunted sounds soon greet the hearing,
 As of feathering oars at night time,
 On the surface of the river,
Nature sees a phantom steering.

Thus beneath the shadow gleaming,
 Of the woodland side and thickness,
 Ghostly forms may ever sparkle,
All with awe in silence teeming.

Here a bark, by love directed,
 Swiftly through the stream was hieing
 Now the moonlight proved the hastening,
Of the lover far expected.

M—2

Moonbeams glanced o'er rippling water,
  Dancing sprightly with the starlight,
  Woody darkness lowered around them,
As they stood where he had sought her.

Still the phantom hovered o'er him,
  Seen by nought except the gloaming ;
  Forth in darkness ever shining,
Patient as though waiting for him.

Scarcely had he there embraced her,
  Ere he fell from her endearment,
  Dead upon the sward beneath him,
On the spot whereto he traced her.

Here Herbert marvelled at the song now sung,
For he had asked for something cheerfuller,
And so he told fair Sybil, whilst he felt
It was a grave and serious homestead there.
Then Sybil smiled, and said, " To thee we leave
More joyous burdens, as from France should come
Appropriate livelier strains."

                              Then Herbert knew
That she, in playful opposition, sung,
As seeing he had sought for something gay.
So in reply he this cantata sang :

      The shepherd's flocks are resting now,
        And maidens meet their loves,

So hushed the scene, o'erhead they hear
  The cooing of the doves.
      Singing merrily,
      Piping cheerily,
  Woo-oo, woo-oo, woo-oo,
The wind is gone a-wooing.

Beneath the sheltering foliage near
  The youthful Mylon hied,
The while they dance he gaily plays,
  Cleora sits beside.
      Singing merrily,
      Piping cheerily,
  Woo-oo, woo-oo, woo-oo,
The wind is gone a-wooing.

Sweet Love is couched between the pair,
  And now he links the chain,
When all the maids and shepherds sing
  A full and joyous strain.
      Singing merrily,
      Piping cheerily,
  Woo-oo, woo-oo, woo-oo,
The wind is gone a-wooing.

Aerial fragrance lulls the mead;
  The dove has sought its nest,
The nightingale remains alone,
  A guardian of its rest.

> Singing merrily,
> Piping cheerily,
> Woo-oo, woo-oo, woo-oo,
> The wind is gone a-wooing.

So ended he amid applause deserved,
E'en though for little stood the trifling words,
Their music and his voice were sweet indeed,
He bowed to Sybil smilingly and sat
Beside her, whispering sweetly in her ear
The charming sounds of admiration fair ;
And bolder growing still in earnestness,
In softening tones to yet more melting words
Spake that, which even in the genuine heart
Is nought, but current goes for all in all ;
Which caused the modest eyes to turn away,
And brought the latent dimples to her cheek,
Oh, what can warm the soul as kindly words ?
Igniting sympathies we wot not of,
And drawing closer to—and closer still.

END OF PART II.

PART III.

The light of love anew the spring-time bud,
Was bursting forth, was glowing day by day.
The germ of love grows well i'the sun of youth,

Refreshed and nourished e'er by tearful rains,
For so the plant is tempered to the gale
Of life's vicissitudes, and strengthened gives
Maturity.   On, onward Star of Love !
Yet wander on, and seek fresh hearts whereon
To send thy beams to lighten life and hope.
Thy beam a staff that striking so the rock
Of hardened life it flows with honey then
And teems with sweetened kindness. Lyre of love !
Oh, let thy music so entrance the heart
With harmony , that every broken chord,
Discordant passion, each may flit to hell.
Fair Nature beareth love to all the world.
Of old two nobles dwelt on either side
Of yonder vale, and deadly feuds were rife
Between them ; but the flowing torrents came
From distant hills and made the placid stream
That now exists, as though to bring from high
The fervent message, "Peace, goodwill, and love,"
And this, the lesson Nature taught, is shewn
By ancient ruins still on either side
The peaceful stream ; now peering deeper yet
Into the darkness of the past there glides
A serenader from the castled shore ;
It is a Prince's son about to woo
The fairest daughter of the neighbouring chief.
What flowery vale would not a river be

To bear such scenes; their union made him lord
In time of both domains, and Nature crowned
Her handiwork in peace, goodwill and love.

Whilst many days were passing, Herbert knew
His heart was moved with fervent love for Sybil,
And having told her so, was pleased to find
Her glad, and then, what times ensued!
They sought Sir Hugh and meekly told the tale,
But no reproof received; though loth to lose
His child's society, he thought how much
The happier all would be, so gave consent.
Our friends were now assembled in the hall,
With cheerful faces, though with heavy hearts,
For time drew near for Albert to depart
For Fontenoy and wealth. The hearty voice
Of conscious honesty possessed Sir Hugh,
As Albert's tranquil eyes were turned upon
His former patron and his later friend.
Amid the converse free, in kindly tones
He asked, how came his son to dwell in France?
To which request he tearfully replied,
That if he told him how, his telling would
Be long, yet still the more Sir Hugh then pressed
The good old man to tell, who thus began
His tale :

"We lived amidst yon southern hills,
Where such the place, if wishes might beget
One happiness, provision would not leave
One aught to wish for ; where the Deity
Of ever-breathing nature calls aloud
For worshippers ; where all in unison
Do act, obeying all-commanding laws
Of neighbourly esteem, and there we lived,
My wife and I, who blessed with offspring dear,
Most keenly felt were grateful to receive
The great unbiassed magnanimity
Of God's eternal providence.   'Twas where
Maternal pride shone down in genial love
Upon our children's joys, soul-mingled with
The binding of a father's buoyant hopes.
But woeful was the day my Beatrice took
Our little daughter Alice for to see
An old but earnest friend one Sabbath day—
The hallowed day, whose consecrated charms
Full spell-bound holds in venerating awe
The pigmies of the superficial world,
Whilst dwelling on the vast and wondrous hand
That blessed it, there shone forth its fresh
Though inborn majesty and holy, lent
Its grace to those for whom 'twas early blessed.
But woeful was that day to me, nor late,
Nor later came they home ; for though the morn

Had broken fairly, clouds incipient
Arose on high and soon became a dark,
Oppressing mantle there, and grew and grew
Until the gathered storm had stolen o'er
Their hilly path.

         "Next day, ere dawn appeared,
I sought them at our friend's, with fearing hope
That they had stayed the night, but there no
     guests
Had been. Oh, spare high Heaven! spare me
     such
Another hour of pain, as that I felt
That day. My homeward path I searched with
     care,
And e'en almost had given o'er the search,
That seemed to be in vain. At last I saw
The dear, dear heart I loved so well, below
The pathway ledge. I hastened down, and there
I found her partly covered with some huge
And massy fragments of the rock that reared
Its terror-striking crest an awful height
Above. I well could see my Beatrice dear,
With all a mother's care, had led our child
Inside, and so securing safety 'gainst
The bare and dangerous edge of rock along
The path ; and then the storm's electric light,

Cleaving the hardy rock aloft, to sweep
The path and depth below, calling my wife
Thereby to her last home and saintly rest.
But where was she, our dear and first-born child?
I never knew, nor know.   Oh, grief! oh, grief!
'Tis when I think of this that sadness seems
To gnaw my life away."

           And ere could he
Resume his tale, he seemed convulsed in tears
And bitter sorrow ; then more cheerfully
He said :

         " But still I have my boy, my last,
Who had been left with neighbours ; him I sent
Abroad, so partly to regain the care
That he so early lost.   My sister good
And kind for aye, possessing generous thought
E'en seeking modes by which to comfort all,
Most willingly betook the precious charge."

Sir Hugh full wondering such should be the fact,
Then rose and paced the room in deepest thought,
Until he calmly from a small recess
Brought Albert there a child's silk neckerchief,
And asked him whether he had ever known
It.

O, the enraptured recognition ! O,
The joy that token caused in him !

                              " But calm
Thyself, my Albert," said Sir Hugh Dalreigh.
Alas ! he could not. " Tell me of my child,"
He cried. " I pray thee now to calm thyself,"
Again Sir Hugh said. " All I then will tell
Thee that I know."
                              And, all intent to hear,
In eagerness they gazed upon Sir Hugh,
Attention, wondrous sign of intellect,
Was now arrested fully on the theme,
Both ear and eye, the agents of the mind,
Were catching every word and gesture made ;
With interest so strained, come weal or woe,
Withholding longer would more cruel be,
Than letting loose devouring hell itself
Upon the nerves of understanding ; so
With careful voice and mien Sir Hugh resumed :
" The solar beams of one's connubial bliss
Are ever shadowed by the pall of death,
And thou hast lived beneath its shade,
And I the same.   In happier days our walks,
That through the vales and round about the hills
We took, were fraught with brightness and with
        love,

And by those hills once straying, there espied
A young and pretty girl, who crying asked
Us for her mother. ' Who,' she said, ' had gone
Away ; had fallen in the storm and deep
Below." We asked her when and where it was,
To which she answered wearily, ' The sun
Was high.' But, oh, how long a time she must
Have wandered, for 'twas then the sun was low :
We sought yet none could find, then took her
    home.
My lady came to love the child, who soon
Became our ward, for no such blessing sweet
We at that time enjoyed.   The token marked
By the initial of our language bade
Us call her Agnes ; here she sits beside
Us ; she is yours."
                    The poor old man rose up
With streaming eyes of joy, as faltered he
Across to meet his daughter, who, amazed,
Had scarcely risen ere they met, " My child,
My Alice, bless thee, God bless thee, my child,"
He said, and Alice bowed her head, and then
As tearfully she looked up to him, they kissed
A holy kiss.
                    Oh, hail thee ! Edmund, hail !
Now happier dreams beguile thee evermore.
Oh ! love thine Agnes, Alice as thou wilt,

As sister, or as sweetheart, take thy choice ;
But love her well, her heart was ever thine !

Yea, is there not a destiny in love ?
Is not the fair one often seen by man
At times when he oblivious is to all
That is for him ordained ?   Hast never dreamed
Of scenes that seemed familiar to the mind
And memory ?   Such may be what we have seen.
Thrice wretched is the fair whose heart is set
By nature on her love, and who shall take
Another love—the one for him ordained.
Thrice wretched is the man who marries her
Who after flies to him—the truer one,
By fate elected.   Haste thee not to choose,
O, Nature ! take thou heed, all will be well.

And Alice went with Herbert and her sire,
Each fond, yet leaving those as fond behind.
Then Sybil often with her brother spake,
When wandering through the many cultured fields,
About her far-off love, and once he thought
Her full of melancholy, looking sad,
So anxiously regarding her, he said :
" My dearest Sybil, tell me, whether thou
Art satisfied with Herbert or his love ? "

Then soon the bright smile came, and sadness fled
From Sybil's softened countenance.   She thus
Returned, " Am I content with Herbert's love ?
Oh, yes, my brother, do not think him all
So wild, so gay, as he would have implied :
Far nobler thoughts and feelings has he than
He always cares to shew, and kindly yet
When seems he most indifferent.   Once upon
Our path we saw a wounded sparrow lie,
Hard fluttering to regain its wonted life :
I took it up, when Herbert bade me lay
It down again, for thinking it would soil
My hands ; but pity worthy of a mind
Most noble, generous, kind, then forced itself
Upon him, as he said, ' Yet, nay, poor thing,
Our care may sooth thee, let us think, my love,
That this, beneath the eye of Heaven, may
Be sent to test our hearts what time we find
Our neighbour stricken prostrate by our path ,
Most sorely wounded ; let us haste to gain
Some crumbs and water, little else it is
Our power to do, but none the less is it
Our duty.   God is always pleased to see
Us act towards our fellow-creatures well ;
For He the more will then help us.'   But this
My Edmund, is but one of many traits
Wherein he oft has proved to me, he has
A kindly nature."

                              " Well," said Edmund then,
" It pleases me to hear thy confidence,
To see thy spirit and thy smile return."
Then he would speak of Agnes, so would they
Beguile the fleeting hours of morn and eve
In pure delight.

                         And eagerly Sir Hugh
Looked forward to the time when Albert should
Return, once saying half aloud, " Yes, yes,
Both long and dreary would a life-time be,
But for the many scenes experienced ;
Though all be ease surrounding us, the paths
We tread all comfort, self may carry that
Wherewith to make a burden of a straw,
And life a sojourn on a tedious road ;
But on the road we travel let there be
Enough variety to interest
The fancy, life may then be made a bright
And jocund time, and Albert's company
Doth cause my heart to bound afresh with joy,
Refreshing the enfeebled spirit mine
Of tiring steps towards the goal of life."
And oft of Albert would he speak to those
His children, bidding them to look up to him,
As one who competent to practice as
He was to preach, might well entrusted be,
As mentor and as guide.

                                        At length arrived
The time when they returned, the promised time,
Ah ! what a future was before them all.
Ah ! surely 'tis a pleasant thing to see,
The mingling of such happy hearts, as now
Had gathered nigh together, so to live
As near the good old Knight as they might find
Convenient dwelling.
                                Merry peals rang out
One brilliant morning, as the gathering throng
Paced gaily-hearted to their homely church,
To hear the solemn tones of union passed
Between the fair and good, for Edmund there
Awaited whom he called his Agnes still,
And Herbert whom he called his Sybil now.
Then as the service ended, merrier peals
Rang out loud echoes of the word " Amen."

THE END.

N

178

THE BOWER OF SOULS
—

ARGUMENT.

PRELUDE.—In the prelude Fael, a soul resting in the Elysian fields, is approached by another, Eon, who was an appointed messenger to the Earth. Fael asks Eon to tell him the story of his appointment and journey. Eon agrees to do so, telling him how he was appointed to go to the Earth.

CANTO I.—Eon continues, telling of opposition to the appointment, and of the argument of a Jew, an Egyptian, an early Christian, a Mohammedan, a Roman Catholic, and of a member of the Greek Church, in support of that opposition, yet showing contention among themselves.

CANTO II.—A member of the Anglican Church takes up the argument, followed by Anglican Seceders, an Apostolic Catholic, a follower of Confucius, a Chaldean, a Persian, a Phœnician, a Hindoo Buddhist, an ancient Greek idolator, a Scandinavian, and a Deist.

CANTO III.—Eon, the messenger, expounds to the dissatisfied reasons why they should agree and end their contention. He addresses them in turn, often in reverie addressing the inhabitants of the Earth. The sequence of his address is much the same as the argument followed before, but he breaks off for a short time after addressing the Roman Catholic.

CANTO IV.—He continues his address to the Anglican Church, the Seceders, idolators, and others, ending with the Greek.

CANTO V.—They now approve his appointment generally, and he is sent off by a voice in the air to the Earth. Incidents of his journey through the outer realm and space, with a general description of the realm. The Gate of Faith, the Field of Dreams, the Plains of Living Thought, the Hall of Truth, the Plains of Light, the Laboratory of Force, the Atmosphere of Beauty, the Nebula of Harmony. An argument with an aged Philosopher. Whence he passes on to our Solar system, when he is caused to return by some occult power.

THE BOWER OF SOULS.

—

PRELUDE.

Therein reclined I,—in the bower of souls,
Ethereal realm by boundless space enwrapt.
Whose courts and jewelled halls resplendent shone
Beneath the Light of Worlds ; where fragrant air
Is wafted through the avenues of spray
O'er arching clouds of radiant gold, that lend
A tone to countless zones, transcendent all
In high prismatic hue ; where gardens wide,
All gem-bedecked with fairy blossoms spread
Give forth such odours sweet unto the breeze
To bear, that ever laden with the scent,
Refreshing, clear, it pours its charge at once
Into each pleasant nook concealed around.
These cool retreats abounded, nigh to streams
Of silvery brilliance, glittering 'gainst the arc
Of evanescent sky ; the kernel vast

Of ambient infinity. On high
In wreaths curled up the pearly tinted smoke
A thousand altars shed, of incense burnt,
In humble worship of a majesty
Soul-known alone ; and purer being so.
Wandering spirits grouped and joyous sounds
Of song upraised, to float in circles far
And wheresoe'er the echoing atoms bore
Them ; they indifferent to direction were,
Since hearing waited where vibration stayed.
I long had known the world called Earth, and
    marked
Its sands with restless footsteps ; now 'twas mine
To watch the world's progression in consummate
    rest
And peace. In confidence I had embraced
The promises by revelation old
Held out to mortals, and long it seemed
Ere Nature burst its many bonds
About me. Here no round of night or year
Was noted ; sun nor moon returned its disc.
No shape existed in its worldly form
And likeness. Shadow, scarce a shadow fell,
For light reflected ; searching, clear, intense.
Grand was the centre seat of it, high placed
And well in view. It shone and governed all,
Transfusing power, and, in part, to such

Capacity of spirit worthy deemed,
All other of its attributes ; and thus
Its presence, love, and knowledge was instilled
Among the myriad willing messengers
Surrounding it.   These then imparted oft
The tidings small and great, the stranger spirit
Wanted ; these mainly were possessed and known
By inspiration leaving to be told
But little, and 'twas chiefly difference held
Of doctrine which e'en here would enter, soon
To be dispelled ; for angels guarded all.
There stood the elders, there stood the prophets ;
        saints
Around in multitude.   And brothers smiled
On kindred spirit met, in ecstacy
Of soul.
                    No earthly form was there to call
Forth recognition : sex nor child, nor youth,
Nor wife, nor husband, father, mother there ;
And yet were all in equal spirit known.
Desire had no existence ; love, but love
Of Light, of Truth, of God, and Io named :
The Essence seated in our midst, from whence
The bright illumined rays came ; there reigned all
The majesty and source of universe.
The Countenance more oft was masked from us
Th' attendants on His will and voice, and which

But conscience heard, e'en sounded sweet and full.
No inequality of age was here,
Nor sere nor yellow leaf was reared on high,
To tremble o'er the sapling's verdant youth.
The spirit knows no difference of age
Nor jealousy of form.   Good will and peace
Uninterrupted reigned where'er might sail
An airy atom through this ocean realm
Of love : the blessed domain of Io great.
Therein reclined I, when there couched beside
Me on the moss-like sward a friendly shade,
Who, weary of a lengthened flight sought rest.
I knew what aim and great occasion led
Him far to journey like a meteor swift
Through space, and knew of his return ; but not
The detail or the story of his flight.
So being yet of recent welcome there
Fresh to the realm and its intelligence,
I then with sympathetic manner asked
The shade in kindly tones, if weariness
Debarred his friendly will to speak and tell
Me all concerning it.   Somewhat surprised
I knew it not, good Eon answered :—

                                         " Nay,

My brother, never shall a weary wing
Restrain my humble voice from praise, or song,
Or other worthy purpose.   It is long

In story, but thy willing ear will find,
Since thou hast sought the theme, no tedious
    strain
Therefrom to wish for silence broken now."

Glad of the answer given, I in joy
And earnest thanked him.   Most beautiful
He was for one to look upon, as though
The influence of the surrounding realm
Had closed combined with habit o'er his brow,
Surcharging all his form with grace benign
And heavenly mien.   He said ;

                                    " A time ago
Happy in all humility like thou,
Or they, or these, and resting here in peace
From days of dubious life on Earth, 'twas mine
To feel content.   I would then praise and sing
In ordinary, but anon was called
Upon to join with others in the glad
And joyous gathering of precious herbs
For speedy sacrifice on altars small,
Our own.   And, oh, how willingly 'twas done.
All eager in the preparation ; soon
Was all accomplished.   Then the incense prayer,
Breeze lifted, soared in volume high and far
The while an elder rose to speak.   He said :

' Oh, Sovereign of Creation !   Lord of all !
Oh, Power unfathomable !   Oh, Thou ! who now
E'en gavest us the thought, hear us, hear us.
It is our prayer that one be chosen, thence
To warn and teach all those thy people who
The nether world inhabit, and whereon
Once stood thy favoured house, in times now past.
We know they have the law and prophets' words,
Possess the sweeter fruit of later love ;
But now when mind and thought is better trained,
And more expanded, fitted more its will
For just appreciation, little touch
Or fine conjunction made, would so illume
The greater, wiser circuit there ; the less
O'er earth would scarce a cloud discover.   Let,
So let Thy Spirit move 'mong spirits here
That with electric compact it shall stir
A friendly medium, there on Earth to cry
Aloud, and call a far-off audience :
Send yet another token of thy love
Enduring.   Neither have I fear to ask
Of thee this boon, for knowing it is one,
With all thy boundless grace.'   This said, the
      Voice
Was heard amidst the seven angels there
Who herald forth the sounds that issue bears
The Light.   Immediately a star shone out

Along the belt of Io's spirits, which
Were unperceived held before the first
And highest band.   This star it was that then
In flashing brilliance quickly sped towards
Me.   Hovering o'er me for a moment more
It disappeared.
            Then thankfully we raised
Our song on high in praise and harmony.
With joy, but in humility I passed
Among the throng devoted evermore
To Io's service, loved.   Nor saint I came
There, martyr, prophet neither ; chosen still.
For me to gather, glean and further what
Of actions might be useful, it was mine ;
For me to honour, love and worship what
Of truth the universe displays, was mine.
In spirit now is wafted far beyond
These fields, some portion of the scents there
    culled ;
But still I knew not yet the order set
Of this my work.   Soon was the veil withdrawn."

CANTO I.

A moment Eon paused.   Then thus pursued :
" My mission opens here.   Gathering around

Me, spirits sought intelligence, as though
From one, who had authority to speak
Of things divine; as also we of late
Were wont to listen to the elders' voice
In love expounding mysteries amidst the groups
Innumerable.   And eager questions then
Were answered readily.   The light was fraught
With such of truth and argument that no
Perversity might answer to, nor sage
Deny.   As hovering spirits crowding pressed
About me, so there came a charm of sweet
Low murmuring music, and then presently
A sound of singing voices through the air :
' Oh ! blessed thou, my chosen, raised among
The elders, go thou to the nations.   Speak
My word and it shall dwell with thee.
Time waits, ye may go, and it passes, then
Ye may not; there is that transpires for which
I may recall thee yet again, and thou
Shalt haste.   Go ye, and speak of what ye know.'
This was repeated yet again, again,
Until the all of thronging spirits heard.
Ere long I knew twas this that proved my work.
About the wider circles stayed to hear
Some freshly entered spirits, some who knew
Not yet what sum of faith goodwill required.
Peace they had found, but still had much to learn

T'enable them to keep it.   Many traits
And worldly attributes yet clung to souls
Received by Io ; traits which perfect peace
Required the cleansing from : this was the part
Of Io's messengers.   But now it seemed
That more was wanted as creation grew,
Discordant views were rife e'en in the bower
Concerning now the means by which they each
Had entered it.   For there were many sects
And many differing worshippers therefrom,
The Jew and Gentile here were placed and met
Full oft, amazed.   'Twas now great Io's act,
Ere my departure for the natural world
Through me to reconcile, subdue, or smooth
The semblance of a chafing jealousy
And bring them back as one in will and thought
And soul.   My spirit now will shew thee this.

The chanting voices heard, at once there rose
A clamour from among the many souls
Of differing sects, and one exclaimed aloud :
' Oh ! shades of Abram, Isaac, Israel,
Can ye not show the power of elders, saints,
Or patriarchs, and thus direct by right
The favoured choice towards thy children ? Why
When thousands here await should choice be made
Of Gentile ? Are we not great Io's chosen ?

Who strong among the nations witness bore
For many thousand years of Io's might,
Of Io's law, ere Shiloh came ? Who brought
Through every trouble known, account to man
Concerning all the great and only truths,
His work, His love and just command ? The Jew
Or Gentile ? Moses and the prophets old,
Are they naught ? What of David, Hezekiah,
Josiah, Ezra, Nehemiah ? Stand
Beside them any hoary Persian, Greek
Or noble Roman ? Nay. Let stand a Jew.'
I smiled at thought how vain the protest was,
And knew the worthy soul would see it erred.
As soon as sacred oil should ease the harsh
And jarring spring 'pon which it rolled its voice.
An old Egyptian here took up the theme.
' Give way, give way, ambitious spirit. Say
Was there not as ancient and as great
A nation as thine own ? Had Egypt not
A God and stately government, when all
Thy recreant people stole away as thieves
Do in the darkness of the night ? What power
Was thine when under ingrate Moses fled
Thy horde of rebels ? 'Twas great Io's hand
That held thee from a thousand deaths deserved.
What effort of thine own preserved thee then ?
Vile perjured people, know the same High Hand

Had lifted us a nation long ere saw
Thy leader light of day.   And Memphis stood
In glory and with temples for our due
And heartfelt worship.   Oh, preposterous
Conceit, to think that Io's face was turned
From us of old for that He favoured thee.
Punished we were, but wert not also thou ?
Thine history is a series of the ill
And dread rewards of base iniquity.
Give way, for Egypt worshipped Io, though
Identified in Oshir.   Idols set
On high to represent one's God and draw
The soul to worship its divinity,
Yet proveth no idolatry nor sin ;
But when the soul rebellious raises vice
And makes it God, there falls the promised curse.
Is Io known unseen to all ?   Ah, no.
When man is taught like Moses and his sires
Perforce to worship the Unseen, then let
His conscience and his duty dictate prayer
As he commanded is.   Yet hath he not
An image even so before his eyes ?
Plainly in mental vision Io see ?
Then if he carve in stone resemblance fair,
His vision true, and then shall set his work
Upon an altar bright, to bring before
His presence daily all he holds most dear ;

Where comes idolatry ? Go, rather seek
It where thy brethren horde ; 'tis there among
Great Io's chosen bands, 'tis there among
A people whom the law of old was made
For ; even favoured by a real and once
Most frequent visitation. Lost to mind
All this, they build up gods of evil things,
Of gold, of passion, and of aught that suits
Their baser inclination.

                       Ages rolled
And He to whom ye looked and sacrificed
Was held the same by us, Supreme ; and He
With us Most High was even He Most High
With thee. When Abram came his God was ours,
When Joseph stayed the same. Availeth it
What time tradition and obedience turned
To myth and lawless symbol ? Was it aught
But Nature's sequence for the nations, far
Dispersed, to lose their history and forget
Their first religion ? Or, when lands were swept
By ruthless horde and fierce foe to sink
In slavery their once most honoured themes
And customs ? What of Perse, Phœnice, of Ind,
And China ? All were once the same in Noah.
In Peleg's time rebellion scattered all
And filled the distant lands with schism. Anon
The fierce Pali swept the east, the north,

And us.   O what surprise remains that faith
Was crushed and Io nigh forgotten ?   Saw
We still the Light of day, fountain of Life's
Most blessed relations, source of all we held
Most dear.   Therein was Unity of light,
Of shadow, life and feeling, cold and heat ;
Therein the Essence and the Spirit.   There
The satisfaction of our weary thirst
And hunger.   Phra, the brightest and the One
We looked to.   Phra, the sacred, holy, great.
Oh, why not worship then this Union ; 'tis
The type of mundane wedlock in her high
And starry grandeur.   Thus we came to bow
The knee to Oshir or Osiris, with
His consort Isis.   Do not nobles, men,
And supplicating nations, for a boon
Approach   the   king   through   her   more   clement
      heart ?
What better time than night for commune with
Our God ?   And e'en on high could we see all
The great embodiment of our ideal ;
Sailing in splendour through the ambient air.
Humbly I crave for mercy if our thought
Ne'er reached its goal !

                        So Isis was proclaimed
Divine with great Osiris ; her, or moon,

Or earth (and erstwhile Ioh called) we loved.
From thence incipient error spread and myths
Abounded.   Fable took the stead of truth
And fiction followed history.   Still we held
The heritage, and I am here as seal
To what I speak.   Though Moschus of Phœnice
Attempted to explain the hoary Earth's
Creation, fast as any later son
Of philosophic Saxony, we looked
The while on Phra, and chained the blackest lore
Of atheism and death, till Mahmoud came:
He brought us back to Truth.   Ay, Faith and Truth
We first maintained an immortality;
And though we sadly sinned, hard punished too
Were we at many times.   Can we forget
The treatment of the mad Cambyses?   Nay.
And yet we sowed the seed of science, art,
And letters, for the peace of future states,
Good kings and nations great.   Didst help, good
    Jew,
Onias build a temple?   Worthy soul!
'Twas Allah gave us faith and truth, himself.
Yea, I have spoken.'

                    " Hardly silence reigned
Ere two of old, who Luke and Philip named,
Together rose to take exception.   Luke

                                    o

In friendly way was granted speech, as though
The other deemed him abler such to make.
With look benign and dignified, the friend
Of Paul then scanned the spirits round.   With
    tone
Of voice and choice of word as culled from time,
Experience and travel great, his soul
Then welled o'erflowing :
                       ' Good thy hearing too.
Dare ye assemble these thy erring thoughts
In full parade before the faithful band
Of Galilee ? Egyptians, Jews, and sons
Of India, Persia, China, all are here,
And it sufficeth it is Io's will ;
Yet how they came, or what their passing right,
There are not those can say.   Within this realm
Are legions who have followed close the words
And tenets of our mission ; those we preached,
Both far and broad, and cast like scattered grain
Before the bristling wind.   The Saviour's death
And resurrection.   Sacrifice and sure
Atonement.   Charity and peace and love.
It grew apace, and spread, though much was
    bruised,
Or mowed, or burnt.   The plant of Nazareth
Thrived, was, nay is, and ever will be life,
And sign and passport for admission here.

Were there not Jews absorbed from ages past
To present time among the Gentile bands
And who have lost, by fair descent, all caste
Of old extraction ?   Some are numbered still
Among the heathen, some are giant lights
And forward leaders of the Christian Church.
What man can tell a Jew when not a Jew ?
Whose fathers born within the stricter pale,
Mosaic law—perchance would claim a right
And favour as would yonder priest, a love
Much greater, dearer than his son of time
Could claim through Io's son and sacrifice.
Ay, see ye not a son of thine, O Jew
Hard by, a warrior—bearer of the cross ?
Think now of him, not as thy harsher will
Dictates, a recreant scion of thy house ;
But as the will of Him who sits on high,
Who whispers of a neighbour, uttering love
By meek rebuke, softly reminding thee
Of sweet a word, and that of brother.   Know
That I may be a Jew, and so may be
This now appointed messenger.   What word
Have ye to say me nay ?   When darkness held
The world, by reason of the thickened veil
Of ignorance, neglect and dire mistrust
Of Io's grace, irreverence walked abroad.
The law forgotten, or unread, what man

Would wonder when the Roman arms and power
Held sway o'er half the earth, that heart and mind
Inclined towards the gods of their new modes
And fashion ?   So the land was sinking fast
In blackest night.   But, lo, a brilliant star
Shot up on high, and lit the earth around ;
Foretold by Baptist preacher.   While it shone
The Light was perfect.   But as years wound round
Upon the reel of time, its brilliance grew
In sudden vast intensity.   It threw
Afar the numerous sparks, that after lit
The fabric of a church ; then flickered out
And died.   That early church it was I saw
And laboured in to save and keep a flame
Again to light the world.'

                              " Slowly arose
A gaunt, though stalwart Syrian, who begun ;
' God lives, Mahomet is his prophet.   Can
It be, that lowly Christians claim their faith
To be the only food and mighty soul
Preserver in existence ?   Lessons taught
By great Saladin all forgotten ?   Is
Inconium, Ptolemais even lost
With fair Jerusalem, all to Moslem power ;
And yet ye arrogate sole saving balm
And influence to Paradise ?   Away with such
Conceit.   Ye have your Adam, patriarch Noah

And Moses, lesser prophets than the One
Of Bethlehem, but we have great Mahomet ;
The highest, mightiest, conqueror of sin
E'er walked the earth. Shall we not see your
    Lord
First offered mediation and refuse
In favour of a greater one, and he
The wise Mahomet only mediator
And greater far than all the prophets ? Where
Then yet is that great boast from Christian lips
But now we heard ?   Did not the Islam faith
Thresh out the base idolatry that Jew
And Gentile both had fallen into ; both
Corrupted unto death had practised ?   Did
It not bring back a proper reverence
To man for his Creator ?   God is good.
Instilling worship and sobriety,
Great Allah loves us.   He is wise and just.
Mahomet is his prophet.   He was poor
And lowly.   God it was who raised him.   He
Was persecuted nigh to death, when God
Assisted him.   He gave to him the sword
Wherewith to turn upon his enemies :
Also the enemies of truth and faith.
Now millions worship Allah who e'en now
Would still be living in idolatry.
Allah is good.   Far reaching, yea, how far ?

The faith prevailed from Mocha, ay, Muscat,
Unto the Gambia's mouth ; from Granada
And old Algiers to Zanzibar ; again
From Europe's Danube to the river east
Of Ind, and from the Volga to Ceylon.
Is it not fair to say it did a good ?
Fair countries there, where date and cocoa palm
The fig, banana, orange, plantain grew.
Where spices sweet, and cedar, sandal wood
Were found, and gold abounded.   Silks all rich
And beautiful to look upon were made.
Such gold, such silk, the old world valued much
When well they would array themselves in times
Of gala, celebration, worship, dance
Or feast.   Whom think ye, that we thanked for
        these
But Allah ?   He is good.   It was the sword
Of great Mahomet spread the faith among
The heathen, taught them to look up to Him
The good and just.   Our work is stayed awhile,
Our empire wanes ; but give us counsellors
And leaders incorrupt, and where are found
A wiser, braver people ?   Under own
Or Christian sovereigns, humble loyal men ;
But lost to all that may be good and true
Where high and chief control in faith is mixed,
Basely alloyed with foul dogmatic schism,

All self corrupt in policy, by side
Misled through individual greed of chiefs
Advising. Know there is a spot on Earth
Where Islam's people live in happiness.
Then witnessing how the Moslem rule is base
'Twill happy be when India shall absorb
The Syrian realm. If poor and lowly (true
And loyal still) the faithful are to be,
There no more humble, peaceful subject lives ;
And he will walk in friendship with the Jew
Or Christian, Greek or Roman Maronite
Or Druse ; but let his fellows governed be
Justly by that same sword and rod as he.
Seeing great powers and systems ordering states,
Partitioned o'er the Earth, devoutly let
Me crave or pray that nothing so-called Greek
Shall hold that rod.'

       " Here latent wrath
Was rising and I would have murmured, ' Peace,'
But that I knew no harm could come, for all
Would lead but to a better feeling there
As speech came round, and quickly now it came.
Hear what was said :

    ' Proud Bedouin, hold thy peace,'
Cried one that erst had breathed Italian air,

A monk and priest ordained. 'Beware how ye
Deny great Io's Son and laud thy faith
In credit of the sword. Our mission there
On earth was peace, good will, and love ; not war,
Nor blood, foul plunder, fire.'

                    " The Syrian glanced
In haste and somewhat fiercely, saying, ' Hold,
Have ye not slain your prophet, plundered then
His very garment, massacred his own,
His true disciples ; burnt their followers ?
' Nay,' answereth he, the monk. ' Hast thou so
    far
E'en lost thine ancient wit ?   Discernment plays
Thee truant so.   No Christian did these things.
Cast thy fierce eye around to light perchance
Upon some poor and guilty Hebrew, rest
Upon a soldier once in Roman arms,
Perchance upon a Roman Emperor,
Or prelate of the old mediæval church,
For even there, I must confess, was once
Corruption ; then you find you those accused.
The mission——'

               ' Speakest thou so blandly mild
Of old and base corruption ? ' quoth a Greek,
' Hast not at Rome a petty god set up

In arrogance as universal head
Of churches ?   And did we not early see
Th' ingenious thought and cunning trick conceived ?
The mighty despot grasped too much, too far
And temporalities fell fast away;
'Twas this o'er-reaching policy that broke
Ere long in shattered fragments o'er the west,
As well as east, and sacred Syria lost.
Oh! what but foulest greed was there ?   Couldst
    claim
A virtuous title to humility ?
Corruption sated church !   In history's store
And old popes' lives there is a sink
Of putrid action as would make a fiend
Of any hell give thee thy well-earned bays.'

The Latin winced, but quick returning said:
' I give thee back, O Greek, thy word. Dost know
The tenets of thine own belief, or reigns
There such confusion in thy doctrines mixed,
That not a trace of Christianity
May be discovered, in the shepherd, nay
Nor sheep ?   So patched with error, bigotry ;
So creamed of all true faith and precept pure ;
So cloaked with gaunt absurdity and fraud,
That none can tell where lies its use benign
Or goodly influence.   And for abuse

Of rite and ceremony take the palm ;
Thou hast thy pope, and mystic vestments, saints
And pictures, ignorance, credulity,
Enough to sink the truest buoy of faith
Ere laid in any world. Corruption, bah !
The very prelates buy their places, sell
A people's intellect and soul for pence
And fabricated relics. Rome has had
Of men the greatest thinking doctors born
Of world, to lead or check its action. Nor
At all times could its fathers take the law,
Or way suggested by a deacon, priest,
Or layman ; yet its steadfast will and work
Has gleaned a harvest o'er the outer fields
And habitat of man. This leads me back.
The mission, I assert, was peace, and where
It reaches far and wide the blessing tells
Of cultivation, art and science deep.
We go to all as bidden, telling them
Of tidings good. Its peaceful silent way
Then turns the savage breast from hate to love ;
From vengeance unto mercy. The quarrel ends
And friendship smiles in honest shame, and yet
Anon, walks proudly conscious of its high
And godlike influence. Good will ensues,
The arts increase and happiness abounds.
Think ye, your vengeance and your hate and war

Is more akin to His own attributes,
Than the unostentatious work of peace,
The slower work of deep, untiring love ? '

CANTO II.

" A silence fell around. The words seemed nigh
To lull the petty storm, as will the soft
And silvery tones told by a good old man
Oft sooth the rising wrath of youthful hearts.
Good will and love have magic sounds to quell,
Like oil the heaving wave, the swelling vein
And volume of a brother's wrath. Therefore
I held me still, that all effect of time
And silence should obtain. But yet 'tis hard
To count upon the measure, grade, or form
Of old world jealousies. For as a child
Will cry for physic given then to heal
His brother, so uncertain man will rise
And take offence when least expected. Yet,
Well knowing this, surprise lit not a spark
When, presently, I heard dissentient sounds ;
And quiet waited by, for here one, who sat
Intently listening, spoke. From Wittenburg
He hailed ; in troubled times he passed away.
'It had been better had thy church set forth

Such principles in ages past.　Who speaks
Of love, goodwill, and peace ?　If love consist
Of tyranny, of greed, and cruelty,
Goodwill enslave in ignorance and lust,
And peace be sold on parchment, or be bought
At fiery stake, thy church hath taught it well.
Small space in dungeons foul is scarce a school
For love.　Goodwill is not of mushroom growth
To feed on fœtid vapour.　Tortures vile
May bring a peace—an everlasting peace
To persecuted souls, but not on earth.
The mission preached goodwill to men and peace
On earth !　How now ?　Sets not the balance
　　　even ?
Why sets the Latin Church so light, so much
The higher in the scale than weighty Truth ?
Cast in the rack, some wooden images,
Some waxen candles, and thy relics false ;
Or try the weight of Papal bulls, thy gilt
And tawdry vestments.　What, will nothing bear
Up Truth ?　Not e'en the tinselled mitre too ?
Then surely there is something wanting.　Take
Them out, and place therein a grain of prayer,
And one of honesty, along with one
Of hallowed name ; the name of Io's son :
Ah ! now ye have it even, true, and sure.
How simple, yet a thousand years had passed

Ere thou hadst seen it ; neither was there want
Of men* who taught it. Say what darkness
    made
Thee hard, perverse and cruel ? Ignorance ?
Thou hadst the greater seats of learning by
Thine ear. Conviction ? Nay, thou hadst the
    Word
Most holy giving thee the lie. What next ?
True honesty of purpose ? Bah, thy greed
Was more for thine exchequer, pomp and vile,
Luxurious state. Truly, I wonder not
Thou hast so many intercessor saints,
And saviours, for thou needest them. Why give
More honour to the servant than her Lord ?
The agent than the Master ? Think ye then
Of old Elijah thanked the raven flight
Or erst his God ? O why, if Mary, blessed
And holy, was appointed to fulfill
A mighty work of Io, she the meek
Submissive agent only, should her shrine
And self be lifted up to ill-taught eyes
To worship, placed in heart and mind as though
She were the object of that work, His will.
Wouldst worship all the mothers of the saints,

---

*Chrysostom, Augustine, Pelagius, Anselm, Wycliffe, Peter Lombard,
Abelard, Thomas Aquinas, Bernard of Clairvaux, Bonaventura. Either
good teachers or were men of great analytic sagacity.

The prophets, elders, martyrs ?   Ask them all
To intercede for thee ?   Thy trespasses
May surely be enough, but Io's son
Is all sufficient yet to take the great
And awful burden on Himself.   Think well
Of blessed woman yet, for female traits
Are great and grand, but old tradition tells
How one of them demands she should be veiled.'
' Oh ! Cease thy mincing lecture.   Trespass not
With words of vengeance on great Io's part,
Half-hearted Lutheran,' Seceder said.
' Art thou so pure ? Art thou tradition free
To speak, dictate, or cavil at thine own
Base fostering ?   How much of piety,
True, soft, and holy, meek and lowly love,
Is in thy proud parade of stately church
And gorgeous ceremony, distant mien ?
Thy cold half-hearted service, gabbled prayer
And sleepy lecture ?   Oh, thou Pharisee !
What good thy showy repetitions ? What,
What went ye out to see ?   A tyrant lord ?
One to command display and silk attire
So rich the poor e'en may not touch the hem,
Beside thee kneel ? What love in rented seats !
How meek the living's wealth ! the bishop's state
And charming palace !   Go, think ye of Paul,
The early church and elders—bishops then.

Idolatry, ye may have sifted, yet
A sifting finer, finer, sadly there
Is need of. In the world not many friends
Drew to me, therefore, all the more I closed
With Io's Son, my friend and brother. Oft
He showed me how His Father loved Himself
And me through Him, nor envious did I feel
Though vast the number of His brethren was ;
For all could love Him for His gentleness.
His father, Io, being great and good,
So awed me that I felt a coward in
His presence, that scarce dared I then to speak.
'Twas then He took me gently by the hand
And said ' Be not afraid. It is not thou
Shouldest fear for they who love Him fear not, lest
It be to do some wrong. Speak boldly out
With fitting manner. He will meet thy thought
Ere spoken, with so great a kindness sweet
'Twill set thee at thine ease, and make thee ask
The more His teaching,'—and I found it so.
No vestment needed, though a raiment white
Would please as symbol of a cleansed soul.
He loved to see a baptised babe, rejoiced
When shewn a re-born beggar, lifting him
Upon an untaxed couch beside Him. Nor
Would He enquire of him his bishop's name
Enough His Son had brought him. How He loves

That Son ! Lord, Lord, O let me love Him too."
Far was the thought up-taken, echoing back
In song and praise.   What joy that ye could hear*
That song ye doctors, subtle thinkers all,
Who lost in learned speculation find
A circle square, a straight line curved, or prove
By cunning argument a point has breadth
And height.   What joy that ye could hear that
       song
That rose in answer to a prayer sincere
For simple love.   No science caused that song,
No thought profound, nor reason prompted it ;
That full and sweet, unanimous Amen :
'Twas simple unrestrained love.
One spirit moved, stood up, an Irvingite,
And asked : ' Who here of this assembly paid
The tribute ?   Who possessed the equal faith
To give a tithe of all and willingly ?
Nay, few responded to our call when hard
Attempted we to bring the Church to dwell
On early faith.   To purify the work
Corrupted, office high transgressed and spoiled
Of most its early excellence.   Brought back
The faith in tongues, interpretations, calls,

---

* Eon often seems to lose himself in rapture, speaking to the outside
world.

And prophecy.   And this without avail,
Throughout the more extensive Church.   And
    why ?
We asked for tithes, for greater faith and preached
A self denial strict, in loose and bland
Luxurious times.   Recalled to mind the words
That told of days to come, and warned the world
Of great responsibilities ignored,
Forgotten, or defied.   We knew that want
Of faith, and scepticism predicted was
To reign in later times, and lifted up
The standard high and made austerity
A weapon of defence, as much to test
The following, as oft to combat sin
And ridicule.   Apostles far were sent
To emulate the early church, and seal
The sweet endeavour.   Yet the clergy looked
Askance, and obdurate held on their way.'

" All eagerly now crowded others round,
To speak, to shew, and loud proclaim the means,
The line and conduct of their heirship.   Perse
Pressed by the Ind, Chaldean by the Greek,
Yet he of China gained the envied point.
Said he :—

             ' I make no claim of prior worth
But urge my voice in full support of all

That he of old Mizraim spoke. Full well
The first nomadic hordes and Tartar tribes
Knew Noah's God was theirs, but spreading far
The cruel steppes were trodden both in want
And fear.   Made fierce, cruel, strange, by dire
And savage life, what remnant of a true
And early origin was left among
Our children's children's sons ? But when the green
And fertile oasis, and pleasant lands
Of promise and of hope were found, the hearts
Of grateful thousands opened out in praise.
To whom ?   The One who gave it, and the same
Who had withheld it o'er the barren steppes ;
The Soul of Life, the Being that our eyes
Saw move and wake to life ; and which we soon
In lieu of better choice had Fohe named.
Maybe the tribes had early gained the name
From Ind ; but as it was, what matters it ?
It was.   The nation rose coeval with,
If not the first of powers. Art led forth
Invention, science grew.   Denied we power
Ourselves.   Ascribed was all to Him Most High,
And great philosophers were held to be
Divine. Confucius so.   The good was not
Of man, and so imbued were all that this
Belonged alone to High Divinity,
We buried man and blessed the gift of God.'

" Great was the marvelling around, when souls
Indignant, and who deemed themselves more near
And orthodox, thus heard the voice
Of China. Blank astonishment and ire
Pervaded all. To think that races wild
All unconverted and idolatrous
Were represented there, was past the power
Of comprehension, and the goodly curb
Of civil humour. Were the labourers
Who first had borne the heat and brunt of day
But to receive the same as later souls
Who had but toiled an hour ? Alas, how soon
Can one forget how tares and thistles grow
Beside the wheaten ear. How what is good
And what is bad may still enjoy and breathe
The self same light and air. And yet 'twas known
How slowly sure great Io works, evolves,
And permeates both man and thing with all
The beauty of His will. Then why should rise
Such envious feeling and dissent there ? Why ?
Erst it appeared in conformation huge,
A vast rebellion far amongst the shades ;
Yet, brother, nay, 'twas but a bubble flashed,
And it was gone, to then be seen no more.
Spoke the Chaldean thus, ' The same with us
Oannes called, we worshipped, and like thee
Ascribed all Nature's wondrous gifts and arts

To Him.   These the Egyptians held distinct
From Thoth ; their learning had advised it. Hence
The sacred ibis flew a type of quick
And flitting genius ; man's.   Tradition gave
Us not to hold these separate, but one ;
And in Oannes centered, saw we great
And patriarchal Noah, father, man,
And master of the sea.   Should one in haste
Declare a country evil or despised
When one of such a mighty worth was called
From out it as old Terah's son ? or deem
It blest that such was chosen from the land ?
Methinks 'twas always held on earth, that men
Of greatness and of honour being born
At given place, did bless the country wide
To which it then belonged.   And long ere this
Was fair Chaldea blest, for thence a world
Re-started.   Shem left not the land but spread
Afar to east and north and south by Ham
And Shinar.   Yet I will but speak of land,
I knew mine own.   The proud Chaldean power
Oft swept the nations o'er for many scores
Of years.   Then chosen from on High to rend,
To lash and capture base Judea's sons,
'Twas blessed not once, nor twice, but o'er and
        o'er
Again.   And what if later on it felt,

Then idol cursed and fettered as it was,
The Persian scourge ; it ne'er could take away
The tale of blessings told.   So I am here.'

" The Persian thus : ' Supreme we Mithras held ;
The Soul of Light, the Light of Day ; but saw
The mind of man and spirit of his dreams
In Zerdusht.'

    " One, who from Phœnicia hailed,
Here interrupted with a voice of pride,
Saying, ' And we in Mellicerta '

        ' Stay,
O, wond'rous rover of the sea, awhile,
Let mightier nations speak ; and hold thy lips
Together, pirate, trader, sailor, seed
Of colonies in one, while I for mine
And Royal Persia say my word.
        Though wrapt
In vast, almost impenetrable, myth
And allegory, we kept the Light before
Us.   Great, mysterious, wild our dreams of good
And evil.   Fancy told us where the fays
And fairies dwelt, and taught us all the deeds
Of Peri good and Dives bad.   This power
Of light imagination spread in waves

And circuits o'er the world, so vivid was
Its own insidious lustre.   Yet we claimed
The heritage.   In all our works put forth,
In spell of beauty framed, the attributes
Of Oromasd were lifted high to set
Example to be followed, while those to fear
Were shown in Ariman ; from giant's swords
To fairy bells, theology was traced :
In nectar cups and honey-dew we found
The inspiration of a life to come ;
And paradise.   Still Mithras was our god ;
And that the Sun, the Light of Day, of Life.
Nor is't for me to speak of Cyrus great :
Who chosen from on High to scourge and slay
Idolators, to break the object carved,
And help to build a temple of the Jews :
Once moved a river's flow, and threw down Baal.
Of him I speak no more.   Renown is his,
I cannot add to it, nor deign to try.'

" Now he of old Phœnicia rose again
And said, ' I would I had not faced the Perse
Of haughty mien just now.   Intention stood
Antipodal ; but, lest I be passed o'er
And e'en forgotten, I remind ye souls
And representatives of powers new,
That we of olden Tyre once held a place

In national renown. When David's son,
Bathsheba borne, would emulate on earth
The halls of Heaven itself, and build a house
In honour of his Lord, he scarce knew where
To cut and quarry that required. Adroit,
He cast about and called on Tyre's good King
To then assist. And he, famed Hiram ours,
Made Israel's King a friend, and praised his Lord ;
Sent all of earth he deemed would tend to raise
A song of thanks or hymn of praise to Him,
The great and good. Phœnice was not the vile,
Marauding thief that Persian pride would make
It, nor a world of ignorance so name.
It was a land of commerce, and whose sons
Erst pioneered the many nations new,
And yet to come, on fair a way to fame.'
A Hindoo here then pressed his tribute words ;
He said : ' With yonder Tartar we have Foh,
And gave him birth, yet Brahma was supreme.
Tradition wild to fancy led most strange.
Old time, as ages rolled, gave birth to rare
Confused and subtle myth, confounding fact
With fiction, which ere long took place of truth ;
Many the legend there that pictured well
The moving waters, flooding waves, that swept
The yelling thousands unto death. And tales
That told of Noah and father Shem were oft

The favoured on our children's lips, and lisped
In pretty strain.   But soon the fertile train
Of Indian fancy warped and changed, by deep
And cunning mixture, fair ungarnished lore
And truth to falsest allegory.   Still
'Twas known the great Creator lived, and Him
We humbly Brahma named ; the Light of Day,
Our fittest type of power.   We knew no more
Of Io than our present senses saw
And felt.   Again the fickle fancy changed,
Supremacy was grafted on the stem
Of human intellect, and Buddha named ;
The soul of art and genius.   Oft transferred
From greater Brahma was our thought and prayer,
And all the higher attributes were oft
Ascribed to Buddha, Foh, or Vishnu least ;
For left to his own inclination, man
Will ever err.   No godly man, nor wise
And faithful prophet, came and taught the word
To us, as did they to yon Hebrew soul.
Left to ourselves, imagination soared
And opened out in lily form, to cull
And grasp what fruits the heavens above
Would give by silence and by time.
O'er Asia life eternal dwelt with us
In doubtful theory.   We dreamed the soul
Would flit to other life with restless speed.

Received we this from Memphis.   Wherefore less
Than man should life in other things around
Possess a soul ?   Presumed we not to say
They did not.   So, what might be came to be
What was.   And thence created life was viewed
With reverence, a shortened step to awe
And worship.   Brahma yet created all.
Does Brahma now personify the Great
And mighty Io ?   Ay, since I am here,
It must be.   Canst define or yet explain
The secret of life in plant, or dog, or man ?
Can Nature so endowed possess no soul
Or spirit fair ? Or shall it be a thing
Or factor of succession fixed in bulk
In value and in quantity to go,
To follow, in continuation far,
From times of first creation until now ?
The plant, the dog and man dies each by each
And sinks to earth to form again its race
And plant and dog and man lives o'er again ;
So the material form and parts thereof
Component.   Where went Life that graced these
        things ?
That thought and ran, that sang or sighed as
        danced
They in the breeze ?   Where went that Life, that
        which

Declares a joy and lights the carbon fuse,
The fibre, water, all, to sparkling beauty sweet ?
It is not lost.   May not the score of men,
Of trees, of sheep, a score of each become
A third of either of the kind, where two
Of them become extinct ?   The life that breathed
In man to grace a tree, a tree a dog.
Not all have young, and fishes die.   Wilt say
There are more plants and animals alive,
Or reptiles, insects crawling than in times
Of yore ?   Where men are more, wild beasts are
    few,
And ears of corn are borrowed.   Trees give place
To bricks.   But, oh, how welcome is the thought,
Great cities fall and from their ashes peep
New blades of grass. Sweet blades of grass ! Tell
    me
Were there not more in Adam's time, or shells
Containing life in Noah's ?   Then to life
Succeeds a life, a soul, a living soul,
If wanted not within its world, why may
It not develop in a higher germ,
And order, just as gas or alkali
That fed a shrub, now feeds the tender roots
Of elm, or oak, or cedar : touching all
Mysteriously a fair probation run ?
Satan became a crawling thing.   An ass

Once spoke, and devils entered swine. 'Tis shown
When now arrived at man this life, this soul
Illuminates the image of his God
And Great Creator now with consciousness,
Supreme o'er all things, able now to search,
Command, and govern spheres of lower life.
Awakening sense and subtle inference
Intelligent, then tells him there is more
On high than even his capacity
Can yet unfold, and he is near to death
Again.   But comes a touch of higher grace
To him if worthy, and he lives again
For ever.   Born again to life more real
And earnest, spiritual and true, man seeks
No more to know.   Yet he, ere this, who fell
Again in death's abyss for awful sin,
Is damned, but if by ignorance alone
May be allowed another course of life.
The heathen so, who never heard of law,
Of old or new, revealed or unrevealed.
Before Old Abram was, was Io's Son,
Ever existing, ever able, wise
And just.   'Twas He who knew a righteous man,
Though Hindoo, heathen he might be.   He lives.'

" Received in wonder, such the weapon keen

The subtle Hindoo used. Self-satisfied
He made salaam and rested. Those of Rome,
Of Anglia, and of Greece, were somewhat dazed
At hearing such a wily argument,
Anomalous in course, yet drawn to safe
Conclusion. So with all yet learned, surprise
And wonder seemed to hold them mute, as
     each
And other soul stepped forth and spake their word.
No dream, design, nor wildest thought e'er drawn
From cultured brain, could overtake the hard
And common fact. One could but blandly view
The flower unfolding, and then dash his dream
And reason in the face of actual thing
Accomplished. Quiet, soul, 'tis being shewn.

' Humbly I claim to loose my word,' said one
Of ancient Athens here. ' No envy comes
Controlling me against the wise and just
Appointment. Scarce I knew till now the right
And reason I was here. Clearer light dawns
Across my brow, and newly-wakened dreams
Pass by as shadows. See I now the good,
The wise and mighty works of Io. Just
And great his ways are; praises full I send
On high the louder. Dark religion came

To Thrace, Bœotia, and to us.   The land,
If Gomer trod, had lost all trace and track
Of early footsteps.   Dark too was the night,
When no theology at all possessed
The heart.   Sol rose majestically bright,
Magnificently powerful, and clear ;
A touch of gladness making all things smile ;
Then struck the earth.   Why did we dance for
    joy ?
Why did we render thanks ?   Or bow the head ?
O List !   Because it seemed so thin a veil
That hid the face of the A mighty ; Him,
Through evanescent glory, gazing o'er
His own.   We worshipped Him.   Then, later on,
The lands both far and near returned us nought
Wherewith to live.   Our ships, Phœnician built,
Were sent abroad to find us food ; success
Crowned patient effort, bringing plenty : Ships
So weighted by the beam, that danger grasped
The helm.   The Nile we thanked, and smiled
    again.
So Ceres came.   Our intercourse ne'er stopped
With Egypt, but the larger grew.   Their ships
Would frequent bring their cereal cargoes full,
To Attic shores.   Ere long a goodly priest
Of Bacchus came, and told the name of one
We worshipped.   This adopted, quickly rose

The massive temples seen in ruins yet.
Teachings mysterious absorbed the thought
Of sages and of peoples, lifting up
The vapours of an old, old life, to blaze
Away in quicker flame, but dubious faith
In new-born error. To Eleusia came
Their thousands alien born, but not till years
Had passed. So Dionysius, Bacchus, or
Osiris, what you will, erst stood the great
Creator we adored ; and Ceres, moon
Or earth, as Isis at old Memphis known,
Was intercessor 'fore her lord. High Thrace
Her Orpheus, while Bœotia, Cadmus thanked ;
Argos, her Inarchus ; whilst Phrygia soon
Wafting away to schism, to Cybele
Bent the adoring, willing knee. Fair Truth
Again gave way before the pseudo lore,
Weak man was e'er addicted to. How sweet
To ingrate man ! How potent is the spell
Of transient lies to govern him ! Now quick
There came the multiplying gods, or names
Of such repeated. Ceres, Juno, changed
To fascinating Venus ; as the choice
Locality prescribed. The Titans born,
Conceived, imagined, floated in the air
By scores. So aerial is the vanity
Of poor humanity. Gaunt shadows trod

The earth, and darkness waved its cloudlike hand
I sorrow. Well, alas, might Bacchus weep.
Yet, though misled, sincerity outlived
All superstition ; what we saw not there
Still hovered round unseen, protective, pure.

" Men too, initiated in the dark
And secret mysteries, proclaimed them good,
And the example wise. Three laws there were :
To parents honour. To the gods first fruits
Of earth to give, was ordered. Kindly love
To brute creation. Good the principle,
The rule well followed, ignorant groups
Of men were nursed to piety and hope.
All virtue, tenderness and charity
Was taught, inculcated and fairly well
Adhered to ; justice and humanity
Impressed and practised. This I see and feel
Is how we claim the heritage. How great
Is Io in his goodness, wisdom, love !
Were these not Christian doctrines ? Terrors too
When lightnings, thunders, howlings, cries and
    scenes
Abhorrent, then were shown to chain up vice ?
Did we not Nero turn away as fit
No more for entrance than an unclean beast ?

Example taught, Rome followed Greece in creed
And temples, myth and mystery, but less
Its good and virtuous spirit.   Some among
The peoples there were good and upright men,
Noble in thought and true, and doubtless touched
By grace unknown, unseen till life came back.'

Here one who early came from Norway, said :
' Roamed have I far o'er silent northern seas,
Bleak wastes and sterile countries, yet I knew
Not how or why the brilliant orb we viewed,
More day than night, was so revered by all
My fellow Norsemen.   As the little link
We missed 'tween rise and set of sun connects
The golden circuit, so theories I hear
Complete the cycle of our ancient faith
And wonder.   Came we from old Perse or Ind
Our mythic story likens, whether found
We God in Odin, Thor or Balder.   Still
Remained to us the fiery orb above.
We had the Persian Foh in olden song
And prophecy of Vola, and their dwarfs
And giants.   There the Peri, pretty fays,
Valkyriae ours ; sweet virgins fair adorned
With charms celestial, bright with rosy bloom
Of youth eternal.   Evil genii frowned
In Loke ; frowned as ancient Typhon scowled :

But from him shrinking we to Odin turned,
Or to benignant Balder, beautiful
And just. To these for succour, help and grace
We looked. To these we had to slowly pass
By prowess. To Valhalla, mighty god
Of battles, bugles sounded ; and to him,
The glorious Odin, passed we on to death :
Yet all the attributes we worshipped then
But those of Io. I am here ; am here.'

' Yet less the Arab's great fanatic power
I am at one with him ' a Deist said ;
' But one God reigns. Whether perchance He took
For some omniscient purpose human guise
And likeness once, or twice, or thrice, must rest
As much a mystery as His far-off self.
He spake by many mouths. And every mead
And every hill declares His glory, power
And love. Glad nature points to greater laws
And preaches sermons wiser than the priest
More often utters. This great source of cold
Indifferent apathy sends to the groves,
The fields, the woods, the soul that thirsts for life,
For pure and living water, beauty, all
That manifests the handiwork of God.
Yet there he stays unsatisfied and falls
Disconsolate. Nor can he kneel to oaks

Q

Nor hawthorns, violets nor roses.   Nay
He sees the all created, marks, digests
Its beauty, but he sees not Him who made
It so.   Mistaken some of the old have knelt
Before the Sun ; the life, the self-same life
As theirs, in all similitude the same
Look on a tree, a tree one sees, no more.
But cheer thine heart, poor soul, look up, look up,
Look on yon blue, look on yon bank of cloud,
And presently will such mysterious calm,
Or dream, or influence come over thee
Thou'lt sing and find a Spirit hitherto
Unknown.   Thou, raised above thy life, wilt seek
To know more of its nature.   This the priest
Can tell thee.   Go, go back to him thou erst
Despised and learn of him the all he knows
But oft can never feel.   He may perchance
Be agent for the passing of the Gift
Or Spirit, yet like monies in the trust
Of men, that gift can never call his own.
But one God reigns.   Am I to say he caused
His Spirit but to manifest itself
At one time only in His Son ?   Nay, nay,
Ere Abram was, was he, but one, one God
One universal whole, that all men know
That each may find in Spirit if he will.
Allow that Io's Son perchance appeared,

The great, the wise exception to them all,
Am I to arrogate my faith above
The world of nations, and deny the rest
Made manifest, because I heard them not?
Did the Almighty care for none of all
The peoples He Himself created far
Beyond the Hebrew caste, and leave to time
By centuries the teaching of a Christ ;
The gathering and the gleaning of His vast
Extensive human harvest ?   Nay, nay, nay.'

CANTO III.

EON, THE MESSENGER, EXPOUNDS.

" It then remained for me to speak.   I said :
' Fair spirits cease ; nor bring thy schisms here
For such endure not.   Here one faith, one love,
One awe of worship, whole, unites.   Deep
Yet soaring high, its verge of plane and arc
Meridian infinite.   Yet Io fills
Each point and line.   Ye enter this fair realm
As erst ye entered in far meaner form
The liquid atmosphere about the isle
Of Earth.   Knew ye the how, the why, the dark
And subtler wherefore, that ye entered there ?

Nay; so ye enter here. That ye are here
Sufficeth then, nor cavil at the way
Nor means great Io took to bring his own.
Thought ye to quarrel while on Earth about
The way ye came there? Or, said one, I came
By Afric, I by Ind, or I by Perse,
By Greece, by Gaul, Phœnice, or Gothic land?
Ah, nay, the end that ye were men was all
Ye looked to; ye fought on other themes.
From thence thy dust-cast soul hath flitted here.
Content ye with the end obtained. 'Tis ours
To order that ye find no other cause
For discord. Know, good Rabbi, first addressed,
That much depends on thee and thine on Earth;
'Tis few obey the law as thou hast done:
Great was thy love of Io, and much
Hast done to make His name revered. His Son
Accepted not by thee, yet hovered round
Thy brow in Spirit, and though separate,
United: satisfied by grace to know
Thou honouredst Him, the greater of the Three.
They stayed aside, nor enjoying glory His
For being true to Him, it mattered not.
Great Io's Son and Spirit worshipped were
In Io. Much thy people have to do.
The which if thou hadst careful been, the less
Would be. For thine the first great law, and firs

Religion, should the last be also. When
Neglectful thou allowedst idolatry
Its sway, there came a power to rectify,
In Christian doctrine. Being peaceful, sure,
And true it was but slow. Thy people blind
To greater blessing it assisted not.*
Iniquity e'en grew the deeper still.
'Twas thus there came a mightier present power ;
Mahomet's sword. This swept the shores around
Of Asia, Africa, and of Europe. Keen
Its edge and strong its blow, it turned the hearts
Of millions unto Io ; hearts that thou
Hadst left to sink in base depravity.
This roused the attention of the Christian world,
Created jealous ire. Their warriors fought
A doubtful field, and thou wert made to see
The work of Io. Ages passed. Anon,
The sword was stayed. The slower Christian way
Was gathering strength, the hand that held the
    sword
Was influenced, and both sent forth its Word
To distant nations, working side by side
In peace. Yet what didst thou, O Jew ? Didst
    aught
To push the word of Io ? Nay. Didst lift

---

*In early times, after the later dispersion, it is probable that the Jews
did make proselytes, but in a very poor way.

Thy voice or finger in encouragement?
Nay.   Still thy head was sunk indifferent,
Morose, or cold and obdurate ; but yet
Thou sawest the work of Io.   That is here
Recorded.   So the three great forces* sped.
Time comes when thou shalt work as well thy part.
Time comes and thou accept'st great Io's Son.
Time was when most were Jews ; time comes when most
     most
Shall be again ; not as they are ; 'twill be
As they be.   Schisms developed apace :
Idolatry held many, Islam too ;
And some o'erwhelmed the Christian Church.   So count
     count
We many suns attracting smaller worlds
As moons around a planet.   First of old
Grew worship of the Sun, of Brahma soon
And Buddha, then from Islam came the thought
To worship Deity alone.   The world
Of Christians founded from old Grecia, Rome,
Or Anglia.   So count we many lights,
And each have lesser lights, as moons around
A planet.   Here there are of each great light.
See, here, here, there, here, here again, there, there ;
     there ;

---

*Christianity, Mohammedanism, Idolatry.

Then none may say that Io is not wise.
Ye do not understand ; but are ye wise ?
Thine eye may stretch to the horizon far
Of thy small world and see no more.   But note
Great Io sees full round the sphere.   Wait yet
Until thou too canst see the same, and then
The comprehensive view will teach thee where
Thou knewest not how little thou wert wise.

They here are those who proved sincerity
Under their several lights, and Io knew
It was Himself they saw when worshipping.
Know, they who perish only see a form
Material at their altar ; nought beyond.
This is Idolatry, and he who prays
To such will die.   Sincerity alone
May pierce the veil and see the Essence there ;
One's lipping words avail not ; 'tis the thought
'Tween soul and soul ; 'tween soul and spirit,
    which
Availeth one.   Mark then how one may be
Of any creed, if he but be sincere
To the Unseen Divinity ; for this
Is Io.   Woe to teachers who have taught
That symbols of a God are such in fact,
That wood, or brass, or stone, possess command
Of Life : deceiving humbler beings who

In faith have trusted : these poor souls mayhap
Have poured their faith, their hope, their charity,
Given their bodies and their souls in trust,
In penance racked their flesh and shed their blood,
With all the nobleness men e'er possessed.
Beauty of soul all lost to Io's truth.
Through whom ?　Their teachers.　Woe to those
　　who taught
The doctrine.　Yet for those poor souls deceived
There is a hope in Io's wisdom ; for
He saw their faith's direction.　Meant for One
Whose attributes are His alone, in His
Great mercy He accepts their simple faith
As though to him directed ; opes their eyes,
Uplifts their souls, and takes them to Himself.
What would'st thou more, O Jew ?　Nay, not a
　　tithe
Of mercy for the teachers, duly raised
To teach, for they, if qualified to teach
Were qualified to search for truth, which, blind
In their conceit, they regarded not.
Now, what hast thou to do, O Jew ?　Convinced
Of great dissension still on earth, convinced
That unity in lieu should stand, thou art
Commanded : first,* to turn to Io's son

---

* Roman XI. Chap.

The true Messiah ; then to purchase back
Thy Syrian vineyard of the slothful Turk ;
And afterwards to work, to gird thy loins
For Io.   This thy people have to do.
The great example of humility
Will rouse the world of Earth to emulate
Thy work.   Reception of the Christian word
By the great Hebrew nations will recall
The many millions, Islam taught, to thee ;
The minor forces will unite ; sects, creeds,
And differing doctrines fly as chaff before
The wind : the Jews be Christians ; all the Earth
Be Jews.   How grand is thine appointed work !
Perceivest now why thou'rt a chosen band,
A favoured people ?   Thou would'st see the Son ?
Nay, not until this work be done.   Thy faith
And thy humility must first be shewn,
O, proud and obstinate !   Thy riches strewn
And cast abroad, to gather in thine own,
To people old Judea.   Then, when a weak
And broken reed, and with a contrite heart
Thou shalt be raised again.   But hark, a song
I' the air ' :

> Hail to thee, O Spirit,
>   Hail to thee, all hail.
> Come ye to inherit
>   Life within the pale.

Soul of man immortal,
 Life, or soul, or shade,
All is one immortal,
 Life for aye is made.
  Hail, hail, hail.

Hail to thee, O Spirit,
 Hail to thee, all hail.
Come ye to inherit
 Life within the pale.
Spirits ne'er are dying,
 Life a spirit breathes,
Life then ne'er is dying,
 Beauty round it wreathes.
  Hail, hail, hail.

Hail to thee, O Spirit,
 Hail to thee, all hail.
Come ye to inherit
 Life within the pale.
Life is part of mortal,
 There a spirit lives,
Seeming short to mortal,
 All immortal gives.
  Hail, hail, hail.

Hail to thee, O Spirit,
 Hail to thee, all hail.

Come ye to inherit
   Life within the pale.
Io is a Spirit,
   Life a spirit is,
Life is Io's Spirit,
   Each and all part His.
      Hail, hail, hail.

   ' 'Tis thus there is but one great soul,
One life, one spirit, which is Io great.
But hark the song ' :
   You are part, we are part
   And everything that lives
      Is part of Io.
   His Son is part, and part
   The Holy Spirit, all
      Is part of Io.

   He gives Life, thus we live,
   Withdraws it, and we die,
      Apart from Io.
   He breathes again, we live,
   His own for evermore,
      And part of Io.

      'O Basis ! great and wise
Of Immortality ! How blessed the work

Of His Creation ! Yonder is the Light
That veils from view Himself, the Lamb his Son
And Holy Spirit.   It remaineth then,
O Jew, that thou perceiving now the means
Whereby thou camest hither, well convinced
The Trinity exists, as all must be
Who sojourn here, will seek no more to lift
Thy voice to cavil.   Learn humility
And leave thy patriarchs' hoar shades in peace.'

A MARCH.

Heard in the Air.

Come ye men of Hebrew nations,
   Bow your heads to God Almighty;
Gather, gather, from all stations,
   March ye tribes to gladness brightly
      Now dispersion's ended,
      Jews and Christians blended,
         For Jerusalem.
      See the nations clinging,
      Weeping, praying, singing
         For Jerusalem.

Men of Judah, hear ye, hear ye,
   Trumpets sounding to assemble ;
Banners seek afar and near ye,
   Hurry so the ground may tremble.

Now dispersion's ended,
Jews and Christians blended,
 For Jerusalem.
See the nations clinging,
Weeping, praying, singing
 For Jerusalem.

Come all Asia's thousands hasten,
 Europe's myriad brethren meet thee ;
Not defying, nor to chasten,
 But to welcome and to greet thee.
  Now dispersion's ended,
  Jews and Christians blended,
   For Jerusalem.
  See the nations clinging,
  Weeping, praying, singing
   For Jerusalem.

View how Afric's children dancing
 Beat the tabor in their gladness,
Whole battalions now advancing,
 Lost is all their heathen madness.
  Now dispersion's ended,
  Jews and Christians blended,
   For Jerusalem.
  See the nation's clinging,
  Weeping, praying, singing
   For Jerusalem.

Now they come from western mountains,
    Ranche and prairie, ocean sailing,
Gathering from the icy fountains,
    Some from southern islands hailing,
        Now dispersion's ended
        Jews and Christians blended,
            For Jerusalem.
        See the nations clinging,
        Weeping, praying, singing
            For Jerusalem.

Gird thy loins and strengthen surely
    Belts and bands when on thy way sent,
Some may link and hold securely,
    Crowding round thee and thy raiment.
        Now dispersion's ended,
        Jews and Christians blended,
            For Jerusalem.
        See the nations clinging,
        Weeping, praying, singing
            For Jerusalem.

Benjamin and Judah call thee,
    Come ye tribes so long lost to us,
*Come and cling, ye ten, nor fall ye,
    Hold to Judah or pursue us.

---

* Zec. 8., 23.

Now dispersion's ended,
Jews and Christians blended,
    For Jerusalem.
See the nations clinging,
Weeping, praying, singing
    For Jerusalem.

Waves the lion blazoned banner
  O'er the mighty hosts united,
Raised their song in heart-felt manner,
  All old quarrels full requited.
        Now dispersion's ended,
        Jews and Christians blended,
            For Jerusalem.
        See the nations clinging,
        Weeping, praying, singing
            For Jerusalem.

Yet lest Satan stand before ye,
  Bring the valour of past ages
To your minds when God fought for ye,
  Valour led by kingly sages.
        Now dispersion's ended,
        Jews and Christians blended,
            For Jerusalem.
        See the nations clinging,
        Weeping, praying, singing
            For Jerusalem.

Come, triumphant Jesu leads you,
   Swell the train and march to glory,
Fast the heavenly music speeds you,
   Choirs of angels sing the story.
     Now dispersion's ended,
     Jews and Christians blended,
      For Jerusalem.
     See the nations clinging,
     Weeping, praying, singing
      For Jerusalem.

' Think not the tribes are lost for that thine eye
Is blind to recognition of thy flesh
Absorbed among the nations of the world,
And favoured upon High as much as ye.
Aye, all will work for good.   There away, there
O'er Earth a greater toleration spreads,
More broadened views expand, to lift the Jew
From depths of intellectual void, and high
Above the dark abyss of prejudice,
To more enlightened spheres of charity
Towards their fellow men.*   Shall Christians be
Behind ?   Medicinal science high attained,
Agrees with Moses' law of diet sweet
And wholesome sanitation ; good 'twould be,

---

* Eon partly addresses the outside world

Patrician leader, Christian teacher, eld,
Wert thou to meet him fair upon his ground,
There teach abstention from forbidden food,
And circumcise thy babes.   Good time will teach
The hesitating masses all, and strike
A chord of goodly fellowship.   He still
May not be able to accept thy faith,
But pray that he may grant a possible
And probable embodiment of Him
Their living God in Christ the man,
And keep the law.   Together all shall go
And gain Jerusalem by treaty fair,
For Moslem power shall sink and disappear
Like the dewy mist before the rising sun.
Watch ye for this to come, evolved e'en though
Indifferent man unconsciously assist.
Confer, confer, ye Greek and Roman priests
With Anglian Fathers, Jewish Rabbis, all ;
Agree to meet thy brother's faith and set
The world at first aflame, to rise in peace
And concord, phœnix-like again.   Attend.

' And thou of Galilee, wilt thou e'en speak
With self-sufficiency ?   He Afric's plains
Have nourished has the truth in that he says.
Who breathed more tolerant of easy faith
And broader doctrine than thy Master ?   What,

R

Dost weep and hide thy face?   Enough, then, now
I need no more discuss thy brethren's speech.
Though   doubtless   there   were   thousands   who
       throughout
The mythic night lost sight of Io's bright,
Benign, and burning essence, there were those
Who pierced the veil of painted wood, carved
       stone,
Or moulded metal, there to see in thought
The Light of Life and Love.

                            ' Fair Grecia's priest
And warm Italia's prelate both should seek
By prayer to be possessed of such a love
As those sweet ready tears allow.   Why may
Not Syria's leader have been sent of old
By Io?   Thou hadst Holy Writ to tell
Thee of the warrant of the sword to deal
The dire and awful lessons of the scourge
For disobedience.   Teachings soft of peace
For peaceful nations ; teachings hard of war
For nations warlike.   Who would proffer meek
And gentle lambkins with the treatment dealt
To fierce wolves?

                        ' Yet truly wert thou great,
O, Roman pioneer, in going forth

To teach the Word.   And zealous leading there
Where yet no other creed would dare attempt
To follow.   O'er the plains and mountains steep
Thy fathers walked the continents in love
And charity.   Good work, good faith ; and thou
Wert loved accordingly.   Beloved church,
O why! O why didst break thy heart of love
And set up stone ?

        'Was it not said of old
That *Pharaoh was up-raised to show the world
Great Io's power ?   Yea.   Then why allow
Not Islam's mission, probably divine,
And for an era wise : the lamp's light burned
With bright and searching rays, piercing far
The   darker   world.   When   Islam   hordes   approached
The fold of peaceful nations they were stayed
And driven back as arts, the attributes
Of peace, were fast developed.   When we see
Not reasons wherefore, say not, 'tis not, but,
We see not.   Io great is good and wise.
Go, go and pray.'

        " As many fell about
To do as I had bidden them, we stayed
Our counsel for the little while required."

---

*Exodus, C. 9.

R—2

CANTO IV.

" I then resumed.   ' Let him who speaks of truth
And reformation mark the words that once
Were offered in all charity to all
Who knew not sin ; for they alone may cast
The hurtling stone.   Oh, grace abounding sect,
Beware ye lose not spiritual grace, nor change
The essence for an idol false of words,
Of confidence.   Let not the sinner think
That verbal trust and cold belief alone
Will save, or that which ye already have
Of grace may taken be away.   A plenty great
O'er other churches now is favoured thee,
But teach them ne'er to rest till more like Him
Who gave it.   Yea, teach love, obedience full,
That so the dead may live.   Life of the Earth
Is dead, but touched by the Spirit is raised
To life eternal.   There was Life i'the past,
It is, and will be.   Life is as the work
Of man, a form of splendour put to use
Of man.   His work is worn and broken, thrown
Away ; but Life, the work divine, was breathed
Upon and fire of life was in it.   That

Too may be worn and broken, yet ordained
Not to be cast away like that of man ;
But like a loan so must be rendered back
To Him who lends.   Of Nature's life I muse,
A work the Master saw was good.   Enough.
Yet should I help thee where I tell thee more
This is distinct from better life on high.
As there is unproductive life ere comes
Productive life, when organs are matured,
So marches life of grace ; spiritual life ;
Here unproductive, there productive, fair.
From some the little is taken away,
To him with much is given more.   A child
May die, the loan of life goes back to Him
Who lent it.   Man the same, natural life ;
But if possessing grace matured, what time
Productive and a gift he puts aside
Natural life, he cometh here to life
Eternal : or is doomed beyond the gulf
That separates the region of the saints
From that of those who sin against the Gift.
He that creates capacity for bliss
Creates the sense of shame or pain.   O seek,
Seek not to teach there is no other doom
Than one's remorse on earth ; 'tis mischievous ;
Take heed, 'tis built on error.   Grades there are,
Of them I speak not.   Some of them you know,

Experienced in your coming, but nor ye
Nor I have yet attained the highest place ;
And some not e'en have been allowed to view
The gorgeous Presence.   Doubtless grades beyond
The gulf are co-existent.   That may be,
I know not.   An incipient life expands
In grade of beauty, so it may perforce
Degenerate or yet arise from thence
To occupy a true position here
Unknown to us, yet gladdening the eyes
Of its Creator.   He would thereby show
His might, and conquer over sin and bind
The enemy.   For what know we how He,
Great Io's Son, did preach to those in chains
That erstwhile sinned ?   What the effect or end ?
How grasps my soul the fuller beauty seen,
The mighty work discovered ! Shall I cry
Aloud what wonder fills me ?   Weep for joy,
For praise.   To sing is not enough.   For song
Is buoyant, light and free.   My soul is weighed
So heavily with tears of love and praise
It seems that it must burst before the throne
Of Him, the Lord, my God, and so anoint
His feet with all the gushing stream the full
But broken soul contains.   I feel I love.'

Aspire with all heart, with all soul to Life,
  As the trees and the hills grow high,
O cast off the base and the dead of strife,
  As the dew o'er a bud falls by.

Yea open the soul to receive and keep
  All the sweetness the Spirit gives,
And store all the virtues in cells full deep,
  In the hive where their Source now lives.

There falls the material away, dissolved
  By the fire of the Life therein,
The sum of the crystallized change involved,
  To a gem from the dross of sin.

Then up, take it up, by the elders crowned,
  On the altar of gold its place.
Sweet incense of prayers will be wafted round
  To beseech the accepting grace.

The hills, the glad vales, and the water brooks,
  As a voice from a harp well-strung,
Shall send forth such chords to the far-off nooks
  Like harmonious thunder sung.

And when it may be the Almighty marks
  The approach, and the prayer and song,
The quiet will be like the ear that harks
  For the sound of a sea-rung gong.

Then clearly the Judge will proclaim the worth
   Of the timidly proffered gem,
Which free from corruption, nor soiled of Earth,
   Is received in Jerusalem.

O mighty art thou Lord, Thine eye ne'er shuns
   Yonder world, O how small to thee,
The lens of the air, and the light of suns
   Can but shew thee how small it be.

I sang, then said ;—

                    ' And ye who threw aside
The apostolic grace and influence,
To wear the haggard look, reproachful mien,
And sanctimonious air ; know ye that deep
And grievous wrong thou workedst far and near.
For spreading insult lightly, and contempt
For what was once a strong and holy thing,
Ye led man's mind to scoff at all supreme
And due authority.   Destroyed the Earth's
High sovereigns, and wrecked the fairest lands
And principalities.   The people's voice
Ye lifted up to mock the hoary heads
Of Io's just anointed and His priests.
Think ye, however weak an after race
Of priests by sinful habit may become,
The grace the Spirit spread of old is lost ?

Ye strike the Rock itself.   Believe ye not
Of prophets, priests, and kings the Spirit fell
Upon in David's time ?   Mayhap the king
Or priest may sin, but still the potent grace
Is latent there, and may revive, though back
From twenty generations it has come.
Yet here thou art.   And why ?   Of little faith
Ye are, yet have ye verge enough.   It brings
Ye through the eras, to great Io's son—
Believed ye grace came on through Jesse's line,
Through Baptist John to Christ.   And then no
    more.
Oh, why believe all this, and not the more ?
Why inconsistent stand ?   Distinctly told
In Holy Writ, and that ye credit well,
That this same grace, all sweet refreshed of
    Christ,
Was fair dispersed among his followers :
Hence through apostles unto present priests.
What grace ye have is only that possessed
By all thy fellow men, not special grace ;
Yet thou art here.   It had been better hadst
Thou not have scorned the rest.   Thank Io great
And merciful.   What time the Spirit wings
And enters man in special grace he hence
Becomes a part of Io, capable
To do his work, record his will, predict

A future time or coming fact. So men
Inspired write deeply, miracles perform ;
'Tis Io working through man. Prophecy
Is part of His omniscience lent awhile
For present purposes.

                                  ' Nor let a man
Interpret far election wrongly ; none
Are stayed from coming, though great Io knows
Who will. For one may be in darkness, one
In light, until the latter hour of life,
And each as free as welcome. Tis the end
That no man knoweth. Io knows that end
And whence it came. The disposition, tone,
Or love that led it either unto Him
Or to its doom. The way the tree shall fall
Is not pre-ordered but pre-known. So all
The just elect are they whom Io knows
Will end their life in grace, and come. Nor yet
Is the creation ended, neither whole
Nor part completed. Still 'tis known what like
It will be.

                              ' True it is that higher love
And charity has come to thee and thine
In later times, in place of harder rule
Fanatic. So it is in prouder church,

Ye meet the more as brothers than of yore ;
But still if bishops were more lowly priests
'Tis thine to bow to their authority.
Or wouldst accept a bishop so he were
An elder called ?   Where draw the line when each
Same office does ?   A chapel or a church
Is still a house of God.   Cathedral aisle
Or chancel, as a consecrated cave's
Dark corner ; but a place to pray in.   When
The heart pours forth be sure the Spirit hears
Its welling flow.   Come back, ye fallen sons,
Come back to thine allegiance and partake
The common grace.   The Church as now reformed
Is all sufficient for thy need, and loves
The meek return of members that have erred.
O rebel son ! come back and kneel with grief
Depicted on thy brow within the fane
Where apostolic grace abounds.   Reform
As oft as there is aught to mend, but turn
Not right away from tenets, or thy mind
From principles, established centuries
Ago.   If once in age medieval, priests
Thought well to cleanse the Church of great abuse,
'Twas justified.   But thou hast set thy will
To bad and dire example.   Mischievous,
It led to schism all around.   Inhabitants
A thousand cities knew, were wont to live

In compact harmony of social life,
And as a body whole kept knit all close
And well together. Seeing what was done
By their religious elders, vanity
Then arm in arm with self ambition false,
Caused some to lead a party here, and some
Opposing them, to lead another there;
A many heads and much dissent. Fast flew
Opinions wild, and civil thought harangued,
Would mock all sweet religious fervour out
From honest men. And thou canst lead them now,
If willing, back again to unity.
Wilt thou do this?

       ' Compare thy faith with his;
Yon Irvingite, who not content with such
As Romans teach, went farther still and lent
Most cheerfully the tenth of all his worth.
That it was needed not is nought. Think back
Upon the flowing wasted ointment fair
From out the sparkling alabaster box.
Think back upon the surplus broken loaves
And fishes small. Enough is just, but more
Is generous. His brothers' work is great
And much to be commended. Were it poor
And lowly, did it humbler walk, it were
A mighty factor in the struggle yet

For equal faith ; but where great riches, pride,
And bigotry, take tyrant lead it fails.
Its aim was good and noble. Its attempt
To so revive the apostolic grace
And prophecy, the mystic tongue and power
To heal, interpretation, miracle,
As then would emulate the early church ;
Was true to grand and highest sentiment.
Alas, too much it then attempted. Rich,
It walked beside the Roman and the Greek,
And gaudy vestment, tawdry symbols shone,
Where simple raiment should have graced the church,
Its priests, and angels holy. Half the aim
Were good, and miracles should be received
With humble thanks, whene'er their scarcer work
Be known ; to seek them is a vanity
Presumptuous, unbecoming to the priest
And laymen of a humbler church. Much pride
Is not an element of really true
And Christian life, and arrogance has been
At once the bane and downfall of the schemes
That hither once have tended. Heed take thou,
Lest yet a church of low degree replace
Thy vaunted greatness, pride and mighty aim ;
A vast community and army badged,
Which hath Salvation for a name, and marked
Upon the forehead as though making good

Prediction.   All thy graces may be lost,
And given them to bless their giant work.
The lowly then may be exalted.   Shall
The mighty be brought down ?   Take heed, take heed.
Thy faith is great.

              ' And thou of China vast,
Chaldea and Phœnice, tis as ye say
Thine own have seen the light ; but mighty hordes
From   thence   have   found   their   doom.   Great
    multitudes
Were swept away by reason of neglect
Inherited of generations back.
*Much sin, however, was regarded not
When old time ignorance its evil sway
Held o'er the people.   Sin enacted then
Was mercifully passed o'er for sweet
Remembrance of the created work
Of man, though erring through a careless will
And disobedient when accomplished.   Times
Far back, when ages like an infant ran,
Philosophers would teach all life was God,
One whole, and but expanded Unity.
Various means they took, upholding truth
And virtue ;   much sincere, harmonious good,
And pious work, was done for thought of rest

---

*1 Tim. 1. 13.   Acts 17. 30.

And immortality.   Their heroes men
Of probity and courage.   With ideas
Of evil, Typhon led, and those of good,
Should not a man of worth be true in aim
For such immortal happiness as is
Embodied here ?   Oh, Egypt, sadly low
Thy might has fallen, carrying with thee all
Thy Afric neighbours.   Thy philosophy
O'er-reached itself and fell again to earth
And nature for simplicity.   Ye who
Upheld the deeper insight in the dark
And mystic unrevealed, and spoke of times
Before creation, where is now thy state,
Thy thought, and meditation ?   Ye who sent
Thy sages or philosophy afar,
To Ind, Chaldea and China east : what now
Remains of thy old learning or of their's
In present times ?   Thou biteth very dust.
But wake !   It heralds something better now.
'Twas but to teach humility.   Bereft
Of cunning thought and subtle doubt, without
Thine old philosophy to beg or much
To cavil with, thou shalt receive and hail
The blessed news of Io's Son, and his
O'erwhelming sacrifice, with greater cheer
And welcome than shall many greater powers
And nations.   Hail ! The day shall come and thou

Be great again.   Yet first 'tis thine to throw
From off thy neck the Islam yoke, or be
Absorbed in Christian rule.   For mark, ere long
Will be a movement o'er the Christian world,
That hard will shake the old rapacious wolf
From out his lair in Afric west and east,
And fire the old dam's den in Europe fair.
Place double guard and raise thy battlements,
Call up thy holy war, and mount the flag
Of faithful Islam round ; and when the march
Of Europe's armies near, go sleep the sleep
Of death, or fire and sword shall make thee.   War
Nor flag of thine is feared now.   Lo, thy blood,
Now foul, shall freely flow to nourish far
The lands that thou hast wasted.   Woe to thee.
Yet thou, Chaldea, and e'en thou, Phœnice,
Although a scene of trouble for a time,
Shalt raise thy horn again and see a land
All blesssed again with plenty.   Egypt so
As well, but after Islam is no more.
Its time will come.   And, oh, prepare ye all.

' Of Persia thou, all powerful, great and proud,
Learn gentler words toward thy brother here ;
For he from Ind, and they from all the parts
Of Asia, west and east, are true as thou
To Io.   Caste there is not.   He from zones

Of Arctic Europe is thy neighbour now,
And all thine ancient greatness, power and state
Is as the field that hoary mowers passed
But now their whetted scythes o'er. Though caste
There is not here, most men of nationed earth
By inclination are divided. Where
A people mass together there will bud
A tree of classes branching always four—
The teachers, clergy, represent the caste
Of Brahma. Soldiers, men in power, will stand
For Chiltern. Farmers, merchants dealing wares
For Bice. Last do come the labourers
For Soder, slaves of men. All nations have
It so, and progress smooths distinction crude
The more advanced the more is one, and if
The spirit guiding it, fraternal grows
'Tis good, but if malicious ruin comes,
If class shall war with class, 'tis war of hell.
So teach good-fellowship. Much work and good
Came from thy land, and marvellous the sure
Development thereof. The cradle nest
Of many nations ; first thy sons o'erran
Old Egypt, Syria fair, and Arab land,
And Pali shepherds fought against the world,
As known. Yadavas and Pelasgi, Celts,
Fierce Scythians and Goths, o'erswept the shores
Of Thrace, the Euxine passed, from thence to north

S

And west sat down by other seas. They fought
And founded principalities. There followed
In train the Sclaves from Asia high in line
Of latitude, the fourth and last great wave
Of race and men. They pressed their way but
    stayed
By force of earlier might ere they had reached
The Baltic, Adriatic, Marmora seas.
Repulsed, they watched aggressive, grasping here
And grasping there the smaller bordering states
All eagerly as weak they grew, or when
As oft occurred they were not watched in turn.

Great yet the good that came of all this work,
These wild incursions, savage though they seem.
In time the faith of Christ absorbed the whole
Of Europe, 'cept, perhaps, one little state.
Combined, yet mixed, these races crossed the seas
Still on towards the setting sun. The new
Land found, a vaster commonwealth grew up
Where now all caste was lost, and hand-in-hand
Would labour priest or soldier, labourer
Or slave. Though slow, perchance, religion comes
To hard-worked people, making homes on new
And unknown soil, the better fitted they
T' accept the faith of Io's Son where caste
Is lost. It is not hard to see this land

Once peopled, sanctified, and fast therefrom
Great expeditions sent again across
The seas towards the setting sun ; to preach
The gospel sweet in China, Thibet, Ind,
And so like faithful children go right home
From whence they came : and turn the dealer's
    doves
And merchandise from out the fane, quick cleanse
The sacred house and make the temple new.
Thus purified, O what a train
Could go and help to build Jerusalem
Anew. 'Twould face the lion as it came
To people Syria.

                  ' What, and thou of Greece
Mourn, mourn, ye men of Ancient Greece and
    Rome.
Mourn, mourn, the thousands that have passed
    away
In ignorance, in profligacy and crime.
Thine argument is fair, but few indeed
Have seen it. Rather mourn for victim crowds ;
Yet bring again to mind the slaughtered rolls
Of fellow beings led to satiate
Debased and cruel rites. Weep yet, and dwell
Upon the bloody floors and brutal scenes
Of thine arenas. More of Holy Light

And Faith's high teaching hadst thou than a score
Of other nations ; living Light.   How used
Ye it ?   Say ye.   How used ye it ?   Ye quenched
It in a martyr's blood.   Yet not yourselves,
For thou art here.   But weep for nation's sake.
Oh, what an awful nursery was there
For infant christian life !   Oh, think of it
And mourn.   Yes, doubtless, I can see
A nobler thought arising in the man,
Who, eager came to view the bloody knife,
The stalwart arm, the tiger's claw, or fire,
Along the vast theatre there.   I see
Him turn with sickly pallor to a friend,
With marked disgust, yet fearing e'en to speak,
Or whisper soft, a single manly word
In protest.   There the victim being flayed
Alive.   He dare not move or speak.   But what !
The traitor looks above.   He sees the sky
And thinks.   And this the thought.   'O Mighty
    One
Or God, or Father, Lord Creator great,
And thou who made the world and put his blood
In man to flow ; have mercy upon me,
A sinner.   Save me from the like of this,
And cruel men.'   Acknowledgment was there
And prayer.   What time was heart-felt prayer
    ignored ?

Canto V.

" Brother, long ere I closed my simple words
There had arisen gentle murmured sounds
Of approbation.   Now, these grew and soon
Became a grander chorus, burdened thus :

Go ye, gentle spirit, go,
Haste thee to the old world so
That thy voice may charm and win
Hearts away from crafty sin,
So beguile the good and pure,
Thence may they the worse allure,
Gain the elders, teachers all,
Trees are dead when branches fall.

Go ye, spirit, go,
Haste thee, haste thee so.

Tell the learned scoffers there
Of the greater science fair ;
Deep the problems let them see
Of which faith alone is key.
Onward then around, afar,
Flit ye as a speeding star ;
Light the way of wanderers o'er ;
Show them what a light is for.

Go ye, spirit, go,
Haste thee, haste thee so.

" Then softly rising through the ambient air,
Still hearing in the distance sweetest strains
Now quickly lessening in their clear refrain
Of ' Go ye, spirit go,' onward I flew.
Immense that mighty realm, and ere I reached
The glittering outer gates I paused to mark
A question, or to render answer kind
To many happy spirits who were quick
To seek a closer place to higher courts.
Assiduous to explain, yet anxious I
To gain the distant goal, I could but bear
The many interruptions.   Oft I was
Surprised to meet with one I knew of old,
And oft as disappointed seeing not
One dearly loved on Earth.   Had that poor soul
Been circumvented ere it left its sphere
By wile of unclean spirit ?   Next I passed
A glad and purged soul who times ago
I left in deepest Atheism.   He would
Have knelt but for a warning hail to keep
Reserve, and consecrate such posture yet
For one whose due was absolute.   What change
There is in mind of man !   It must be good
It is so.   If 'twere strong, unwavering,
Constant ; small hope there were for ignorance
And vice.   That were but common instinct ; mind
Of animal, not as a man's, whose mind

Developed to a soul can reason, hope,
Command, and venerate. This is the type
And image of his Maker. He in this
Superior is to all created things.
The soul or spirit comprehends a soul
Its like, and comprehends the theory wise
Of greater Power. 'Tis universal part
Of Io, therefore where is man is He
Where'er life is, is He, yet not the same
In type and image. Many spheres of life
There are denied this honour done to man.

Anon I heard a sound of busy wings,
And presently I saw a company
Of angels bearing in their midst a man
Of aged aspect, beautiful to view ;
Such peace, benevolence and calm reigned there.
The bearers sang :—

　　O come and rest thy weary feet,
　　　　Our Lord awaits his own.
　　Come thou, and couch by Jesus' seat
　　　　And by the Great One's throne.

　　Well done ! thy faith a thousand more
　　　　Inspired to follow here ;
　　O, dear one, wake, thy journey's o'er ;
　　　　A peace unknown is near.

Hear how the tuneful welcome sweet
　Swells through the radiant air,
In ecstacy are all to meet
　A soul whose life was fair.

Peace, peace to thee ! Oh ! gentle heart !
　Rest thee a well earned rest,
Now but to praise remains thy part
　For aye among the blessed.

　　　　" Thus cheered so happily,
Appreciation rose all o'er his brow,
Like sweet peach blushes o'er a maiden's face.
Enquiring then of those about him who
He might have been, I gained for answer curt
And simple, 'One who good was living ; good
In death.'   No more, so went I on my way.
Nor had I gone in full compliance with
My loved commission far, ere streams of light
Shot the meridian high.   Delight came o'er
Me as blaze after blaze enriched the scene.
Resounding music filled the air with songs
As of vast choirs intent on vying with
Reverberating thunder.   Dense the crowd
Of angels passing.   Curious awhile
I hovered by.   Still on, and greater grown
Each instant, yet the demonstration passed.

No thunder harsh or grating to the ear.
But clamour equal to its compass loud,
And searching ; sweet withal and beautiful.
Twas then I stole me closer, marking cause
Of such a great announcement.   Bore they high
In glee a man whose age was that between
The young and old.   Soon gathering all that could
Be told, I learned that he had had his cup
As full of sin as youth could fill ; yet now
Had come repentant seeking Jesu.   Him
He found.   This was the joy.   Such the return.
Rising again, I sped me onward full
Of thought rejoicing.

                "Hurrying ere long
I met two more whom Faith embraced by Hope
Would picture.   Shyly speaking to me one,
With stranger consciousness, enquired if soon
Encouragement would beacon them to cheer,
As time and distance fettered hope.   Far flown
Their coming.   Glad t'encounter such request
I answered thus :

              ' Fair yet thy portion rests
About thy brow.   Thou art within the realm
But barely crossed the boundary.   Here are set
A numerous angel host, faithful to serve,

To guide, protect and guard with careful watch ;
They help the weary and the wandering,
And soon arrested would have been thy flight :
But meeting one who other work has yet
To do, so let him now refresh thy soul
With sweet encouragement.   Thy winged strength
Will bring thee first, upon thy guarded way
Long narrowing unto the Gate of Faith.
That, none but Saviour known can enter by.
Another gate that whilom stood was known
As that of Law, though oft Obedience called.
Still may it stand erect but little used.
Ye known of Io's Son will pass by Faith,
Mark well the beauty of it.   Treading o'er
A blue-grey ether soft, thy mirrored eye
Will then reflect unto thy sense the Gate ;
A vast prismatic arch set all around
In cloud-like folds of deeper, cooler grey,
The portal rose, with tracery of gold ;
Through which fair colonnades of varied hue
Etherial show.   The red gate opens wide
At word of Faith, and angel guards soft clothed
In tender tints all throng around in praise.

' Then having passed the gate, the grey dissolves,
And golden light obtains.   A far more grand
Extensive view unfolds itself within.

The colonnades are fan-like, stretching far
And intersected by fair avenues
All circle half-determined.   Genial warmth
Is everywhere, and all partake the glow.
What time Arcadian pleasure joyed the heart
Of jocund peasant, classic youth, or maid
In simple garb, was barrenness and dearth
Compared with happiness herein.   Beyond,
And further, quick conducted find you more
Of wider beauty.   Far as eye can reach,
And yet but flap of spirit's wing, expands
A billowed plain of softest down of bird
O'er which a web of unsubstantial silk
Is smoothed by unknown hands, a gossamer
That but for lighter air would disappear.
O'er this is shed a twilight tint of green
And ruby rays all intermixed in line
And volume undefined.   Suspended oft
Are canopies of deeper tone, as though
The light were cast athwart through darkened lens.
These but a resting place for weary wings ;
There thou wilt wait, till summoned onward yet,
And yet, and yet.

                    ' This region first, is called
The Field of Dreams.   Here resting, all thy
      dreams

Of yore recur in vivid force, unless
Full   strong   in   faith,   for   then,   the   base   are
    barred ;
But thou, if weak in Faith, had better keep
Thy wing and flight, till gained the distant plain
Beyond.   But rest, and thou wilt know the cause
And reason, time and meaning, of a dream
Forgotten ; but recorded.   Why it seemed
When erst thou dreamed it, that 'twas dreamed
    before.
The place and persons all familiar.   What
Disturbed thy mind to think of unknown scenes
And faces, what bestirred it to recall
And make to live the dear one gone, or slay
In vision friends that lived.   All this but part
Of thine annealing.

                          ' Passing onward next
Wilt come to plains illumed with silvery flash
Of light, but toned to thine endurance small.
These   are   the   Plains   of   Living   Thought.   From
    thence
All origin of genius on the Earth
Speeds as an arrow barbs the empty air,
To find its sheath in mortal brain.   And there
Wilt learn far more than ever learned before,
Yet knowledge measured by capacity,

While granting its equation, will absorb
Thy latent sense.   First thoughts that made the
    man
A power ; a leader of his race or head
Of clan ; a pioneer in science, art
And literature, will now be known again :
As well as thoughts that are in waiting yet,
Or still to be discovered.   There, is seen
The emanation of a kindly love
And sympathetic glow where poverty,
Distress, or pain demands a warming ray
Of comfort.

              ' Thence far shoots the gleam for man
To cradle and to foster into high
Mature ennobling charity.   Thence comes
The child of fancy lulled to rest an age
In letters ; or harrowing problem threshed
From out the husks of ingenuity.
And when a long premeditated deed
Has culminated to an action prompt,
Thence comes the thought resilient from itself
To seek a hiding place in shame, remorse
And sorrow.   Thence the sweeter thoughts that
    come
When all our better self has drifted far
At sound of charming music, and enwrapped

Its being in a weird identity
Most strange and difficult to fathom.   Lone
And lost but beautiful withal.

                                                   ' Beyond
Perforce directed wings, though fresh sustained
By deeper kindled thought, arrive before
The grandest architectural pile designed
In any era yet.   Triangular,
Unique ; no fane on earth can be recalled
As similar in part thereof or whole ;
Unless its carbon crystal substance bears
Resemblance to the diamond below,
Bright glistening in a sun-bathed light.   Its base
Lay deeply pillowed in the varied hues
Of softest heather tones.   Its columns rise
In fair proportion, bearing pinnacles
And towers arched, to grandly balanced breadth
And elevation.

                             ' This, the Hall of Truth,
Is subdivided from its centre there,
Where stands a golden altar and a bar.
Thus forming with its outer angles far
The area of three spacious courts.   'Tis there
That Purity conceives its presence sweet,
Distils its essence rare, and sends it forth

To burn an incense o'er the clean of heart
And mind. Morality, the second court
Nigh swells to bursting pressure, as its valve
And worldly requisition is but small.
Yet, there forsooth 'tis stored in vast accume.
The third is Reverence, a court much used
As thousands of its devotees absorb,
In quick participation, spirit sent
Abroad, afar, around. As class and class,
And grade and grade, all mingled far and near,
E'er need it. Whether it is used for ends
Yet other than legitimate or no,
It must come back to its Creator here.
Ay, much advantage is obtained by souls,
In fleeing upward, passing through this court;
And then the second and the goodly first,
For all commune within the golden ring.

' Passing again beyond the Hall of Truth,
For e'en the deepest themes and problems dark
In old theology acquire a fair
And early shape and uniformity,
One reaches out upon the broadened Plains
Of Light. 'Tis there the pennant of the wing
Must be outstretched in quicker flight. Yet
    haste
Thee to o'ershadow with its netherdown

Thy vision from the light.   All source of heat
Is here, and every form of fickle light
And deep intensity the plains comprise;
So thou shalt quicker go.   Look not around
But let anticipation pilot thee.
Stay not.   Electric and magnetic force
Is first engendered here.   Yet, fear thou not
If well enveloped with the essence sweet
From courts below; no conduct shalt thou give
To currents hovering through the plain.   But
    haste
Ere that sure essence wings as well.

                                        ' Now led
Unto the Laboratory of Force, thy flight
May be of slower pace.   There gravity,
Attraction, motion, pressure, and relief
Thereof, are first ideas.   The source of **weight**
And measure ; chemistry all governing :
Geology resulting.   Quantities
Adjusted ; motion, pressure there restrained,
Or here accelerated.   Alkali
And acid, placed and mingled, where to be
In animal, or plant, or glittering gem.
There too the sweet vibration causing sound ;
Th' incipient chords of music dwell, a charm
Upon the ear.   'Tis grateful to abide

A little here.   The senses all are formed
From the embryo, or the hidden germ
Unto the perfect sense.   Surrounded there
By perfumes, that but add a chain of joy
To the already bounden captive sense,
One hears a sigh of harmony ; a breath
Of music, such as one might wish would raise
And bear him to eternity.   To dream
'Tis easy, that thou art already there ;
Yet 'twill be hushed and lost a time to thee
Until the Source is reached.   What kinder grace,
What better harbinger of beauty fair
Than music soft ?

      ' Howe'er, to soar thy part
Remains.   Onward ; and music is no more,
Left for a higher theme.   Thou presently
Wilt come to regions yet more beautiful,
E'en more elysian yet ; surpassing wit
Of earthly savour so to comprehend.
For lo ! the Atmosphere of Beauty bathes
The wondering subject on the soaring wing,
In all the varied colours blended through
The ages past.   Ay, there the eye may roam,
Not only o'er the hues all known on earth,
But o'er resplendent tints and semi-tones
Appearing in the realm itself.   And form

           T

Obtains a height of beauteous curve and line
Unknown to mortal ken.　Think not I show
That hue and colour hath preceding place
Of light, for thine experience as it grows
And gathers weight, will tell thee how these
　　plains
And pleasant gardens do but radiate
Around the Source in circling balance nigh.

' But here the very thought of form and hue
Hath first essay.　The yellow emanates
From light, as colder judgment from a king
Deciding from his seat o'er what is wrong ;
A symbol of the Godhead, power and might ;
But ere deciding aught, comes there a rush
Of glowing rose, of fervent charity ;
And so intense a warmth of brotherhood
Were justice like to lapse, were not a veil
Of cooling ether and of liquid blue
To warm the one‾and tone the other o'er
As soon to balance both.　So trefoil like
They come together forth.　Combine to glow
Throughout the field of Nature's fancy fair
Or fill apparent void with beauty.　What
Do colours not invest ?　Can mind or thought
Imagine world without them ?　Nay dear soul,
It is not that they must be.　As the staff

Of blackest ebony, or blossom pure
Of snowy white, shall change not in the light
Of sun ; so might the thousand hues of earth
And nature but be white or black.   Think then
And all thy senses war not, what of praise
Is worthy so much pleasure.   There besides
Is form of joint and vertebræ, of curve
Or angle varied, lens of eye, and hair
Of bee's foot, feather down, and scale of fish ;
The form of wing and fin, of orchid, rose,
And sea anemone, alike of toad
And goodly horse ; the form of leaf and tree,
Of scorpion's fang, of lily sweet, the snake,
And that of man and woman fair.   Knew ye
That centipedes were beautiful, or lost
Ye chance of viewing them ?   Misled perhaps
By unfamiliarity.   These things,
However much to earth they appertain,
Have had their forms incipient there designed,
And there developed.   So, the Atmosphere
Of Beauty sheds its charming spirit o'er
Fair Nature's work, and so adorns a world.

' Then leaving this behind thee ; with perchance,
As much regret as thou wert wont to leave
The soothing cadence of the music passed ;
Soon will appear, as nearing now the Source,

The Nebula of Harmony.   'Tis there
Where   rest   awaits   thee.   Ay!   the   goal   of
        dreams,
Of faith, of truth. Much aid of force, of light
And beauty, will have tended to secure
It.   There find Law and Order and of all
That is ; a combination sweet withal.
More oft perhaps 'tis named the Bower of Souls.
Thy coming will be heralded by all
With much acclaim.   On high there gleams most
        bright
The Light and Source of all.   To hear the voice
›Tis possible ; to see the more 'tis not.
That is reserved.   Wouldst learn the more of
        sweets
Elysian, go thy way.   Well may ye fare
Now hie ye quickly.

                    " Spreading wings again
We now departed on our separate way.
For time of short duration all was fair
And clear ; and swiftly rest refreshed I flew.
It was as though my soul was lighter yet,
As mortal kens the feeling of a morn
Of cooler air, all lit with sunny rays ;
More elevated may be, ne'er-the-less,
'Twas like unto it.   Presently I marked

The gathering vapour rolling round below,
And rising, spread in front of me.   I knew
At once that vivid flash and awful sound
Of far reverberating thunder clang
Would then succeed.   Close conscious of the
    cause
I, heavenly armoured, onward went.   With awe,
Yet safely joyous midst the deafening din
And blue-hued lightening now that forked the air,
I kept my way.   Upon the cause I came
Ere long.   It was a woman's soul whose flight
Was   slow   and   laboured.   Though   protecting
    guards
Were by she knew it not and cleft the air
Apparently alone.   Her troubled face
Depicted one in abject fear.   I learnt
From one attending her that she had been
The cold, irreverent, careless wife, of one
Who greatly feared his God.   She, not so vile
As now deserved a separation, was ;
By his sweet sanctifying influence,
Now being brought by indirecter way
Towards the all annealing grace.   Nor ill
Was she as wife to him, for truly good
Was she accounted there on Earth ; all true,
Obedient and industrious ; but without
The warming spark of heavenly fire and love.

Now she it was who on her troubled way,
Would, ere she neared the Gate of Faith, have
    cause
Profound to thank her lord and claim in prayer
The harbour safety of the realm.

                              " Still on
I kept and quickly passed through air disturbed
So fretful for its burden.   Souls there were
Of doctors and divines, and souls of those
Who had been warriors both by sea and land ;
The worker of a craft, the delver, who
Had lived all night, all day, deep down the mine.
And great the peaceful number of that class
Who till and toil upon the land.   These men
Who dressed the land were doubtless favoured
    much
As though the charge and trust all theirs had been,
To keep, to guard, improve the beauty fair
And usefulness, of what the greatest Hand
Had made ; and grand it was to see the beam
Of love so balanced o'er the different grades
Of men, that once at least and once for all
They were in fellowship.   If lowlier place
To some were given, yet, the units dwelt
All conscious that the one was merited,
The other scarce deserved.   Not tarrying

To speak to all, I suddenly became
Aware, the view around was not of heaven ;
The sweet elysian fields I knew were masked
Though great the beauty that replaced them.

" High,
And on my left a giant screen of cloud
Hung in the air, with scenes I knew of old
Thereon depicted.   Lo, a vast mirage.
I gazed in wonder, almost dreaming wings
Had played me truant ; that I had arrived
Unknown, so soon on Earth.   The domes, the
        spires,
Embattled palaces ; a city's wealth
Of ships, of mansions, and of monuments.
And there as in a radius sided line
A view of landscape plains extending wide,
All fresh with verdure gleaming 'neath the sun.
And there again a scene of other towns
Far distant, ether clouded.   Quiet reigned,
Or seemed to reign, and all bespoke of peace.
How gratified I was to see it so !
Not that fair lands and peace would tell of love,
Or reverent obedience, for I knew
That much iniquity was possible
E'en in the prosperous epochs of a world ;

Still glad I felt that peace seemed there.   'Twas
    cause
And base for people to be good and wise,
And so more thankful.   As, alas, about
To reason further, and to store the way
And means thereof, surprise fell o'er the light
Of all my subtle thought, extinguishing
Its brilliant gleam as water will a fire.
The lent reflection of a scene on Earth
Had quick dissolved, and but a mist appeared
For many moments.

                   " Then like zephyr waves
That cheer the sickly pallor of a face
Which erst had fainted, came a roseate hue
I thought to joy me.   But fast as it swelled
I bowed aside with horror.   There, mirage
Again with fell distinctness shewed me war.
Irregular and curved were lines of red
And bright as rivers shone ; and gory fields
Portrayed in striking contrast, by the green
Of meadows left untrodden yet by ranks
Of fierce soldiery.   Much smoke and fire,
And falling towers shewed a ruin great,
As yet untold.   These things of moving weight
Perforce engaging all my eager gaze,
Then nigh arrested me.   Fair peace had flown

To leave the world in bloodshed and it seemed
In dread calamity.   A something white
Oft hovered o'er the scene, but man, or horse,
An orient frock, or flowing surplice wave,
I could not gather to my eye so sure
As to identify.   But now again
It clouded o'er, and left but likeness fair
And close to sheer reality.

                  " 'Twas then
I thought to double speed, and so to catch
Fore-running moments by the heel and clip
Their wings.   But, ere the thought took certain
     shape
In braver action, high a glorious view
Appeared ; this time the scene was counterpart
Of that at first I saw.   A landscape sweet
And beautiful, e'en simulating more
A grand terrestrial glory, and for man
A more triumphant crown and course of peace.
Between two hills a valley swept.   On one,
And on the very verge, a wall of stone
Of massive nature or construction reared
Its sombre strength.   Beyond, another hill
Kept guard as man will guard a treasure.   Great
In number were the buildings, and new built ;
Bright glittering all beneath the mid-day sun.

Though full the city teemed with mortal souls
Yet thousands 'more in concourse came. They
  streamed
O'er hills and vales, they streamed o'er desert
  plains,
And sailed a fleet of ships. All hand in hand
In peace, in plenty, and in love, the throng
Would gather, gather still. The lands around
Were bright with harvest tints, and village nests
An over-crowded colony had made.
That peace was there the many altars told,
All open to the sky, with worshippers
Around them. And that plenty reigned was seen
By much of gleaming gold. The silver there,
Though great its white reflection, was by far
Of less account, as where the heavy rains
From clouds above caused overflow, 'twas that
That led its way to safer reservoir
By sinuous paths. The quantities of gold
Would speak of richer fields than I had known
Discovered, for the largest temple stood,
Cathedral shaped, a solid mass of it.
So though I could not mark the detail close,
I saw what told of one great common weal,
One common work, that all were then engaged
In. Catholic towards a purer good.
The scene dissolved. I saw no more, and pressed

My breast aslant the wind.

" How beautiful
Could men be brought to act with one idea !
Combined to work for one great good, for one
All, all absorbing theme in sweet accord ;
'Twere nearer heaven. But how ! the man
    adult
With scores of fancies, likes and dislikes old,
With taught convictions, prejudices rank,
Could never tack his sail to such a breeze,
Or bring his bark to such a harbour. List !
'Tis not a generation, one, or two,
That may ; but if a child is taught to scan
And so regard the future good, his sons
Will lose the old world rule, and be henceforth
Confirmed in this the better principle.
If this be then to raise or level up
The more debased, or bring down harsher
    minds
And incongruities of would-be men,
It is at least a purer, nobler aim,
Than meanly scoffing at a higher caste,
Or spurning what is lower. Caste will cease
By force or voluntary deed. Shall man
With God-like reason then elect to dare
The dread alternative of bitter force ?

Alas! an answer comes not yet; nor I
Am given to say.   No worldly social quest
Herein is pending, but a thing of real
And utmost moment to the soul.   I would
It   were   on   earth   considered   more.   This
      thought
Erst quivered in the case of earnest wish
And inclination was in arrowed flight
Then hovering o'er its goal.   O that the verge
Was wide enough, the telling bow was strong,
      And elbow angle true!

                              " The radiant air
Was now more clear, and soon I overtook
My   average   flight.   I   journeyed   long   through
      time
In sweet enjoyment of a reverie soft
And soothing to an anxious soul who had
A doubtful task before him.   Darkness drew
Around, which, as I knew not night on high,
I felt was then a stranger incident;
But blacker, denser still it grew.   A few
More quickened strokes upon the shadowed air
Brought   me   to   flickering   lights   as   though   in
      search
Of something fallen.   Soon distinguished, there,
I saw a throng of mourning spirits, dressed

Apparently in soft monastic cowl
And habit ; carrying lamps antique and chained
As censers.   Much resemblance had they all
To old Carthusians which sometime walked
The   Earth.   A   psalm   they   sang ;   one   from
    among
Those of the Psalmist old and best.   It was
The " Miserere mei, Deus," which
Then sounded sweet and quaint.   Still curious
For any good, I sought the searchers' quest.

'Twas one of many bands of pioneers
Who voluntarily helped and looked for souls
Who strayed, required sustaining light and wing.
And often they would seek their old world friends,
Or such as they expected.   This would end
Most frequently in saddest circumstance
And   utter   disappointment.   Then   it   was   they
    mourned.

The psalm they sang would often be the means
Of   saving   wing-wrecked souls.   No   soul   was
    lost
When it had come e'en nigh the realm.   This
    was
But one of many ways whereby the weak
Were oft assisted.   Now they mourned.   For one

Found not his son, and one a brother loved ;
A sister one had missed, a father, wife,
Or daughter was not found ; a mother one,
A husband yet another lost. To one
I gave what glad intelligence I could,
And told the aged spirit that I passed
His daughter many moments since. Then rang
From all a peal of such rejoicing song,
That fair I thought the darkness would have gone
For shame of inconsistence being pressed
Upon its visage. Then, Te deums sung,
They went their way still mourning for the rest.

" Ere long the light to me was present ; so
I hastened onward once again. The way
Was   joyous   pleasure.   Many   leagues   were
        passed.
Yet ere the boundary of the glorious realm
Of light and ambient warmth was reached, the
        sum
Was great indeed. And presently I stayed
Me when I saw a crystal fountain by,
And bathed the warmer portion of my wing.
About to move away, I marked a soul
Of aged aspect there reclining by,
And quietly regarding me. I said :— ..
' Fair paths to thee, O spirit ! Wilt now say

Or who thou wert, or who thou art ? I yearn
To know all aught I do not.'

                                          ' Nay, ' said he
' Let it suffice that well I know the all
Thou art, and what thy mission is. Go ye
As bidden. I once knew ungrateful Earth
And smile ; but smile in sorrow for thy work.
How visionary : Dost think that hard world men
Will look aside from any old pursuit
In curious science, or attractive art ;
From lying literature, or gambled gain
In traffic ? Tis chimerically absurd ;
Impossible. I knew the world of old.'

" I said : ' Whoe'er thou art, O spirit dare
Not say the mission is ignobly launched
Or ill conceived. No rank conceit, nor vain
Presumption ; idle vanity nor pride ;
Surrounds the mission sent, or sender. Sent
All humble I to do the bidding. He
The Sender is beyond, or you, or I.'

' It may be that I spoke too rashly ; yet,
I knew the world of old. You are but born
Of centuries, while I of thousands boast.
And who will listen to a boy ?'

'Nor boy
Nor man will ask them ; for it is not I
Will tell them hearken ; 'tis but mine to go :
And He who sends it, taketh care His own.
But why without the realm ?'

'To tell thee sure
That thou wilt never reach the world called Earth.'

'Or rather that thou hast ne'er reached the realm.
But if thou knowest this, why cry aloud
Of foolishness and vanity ?   If man
Is not to hear, why think that he will spurn
The hearing ?'

'Said I that he would not hear ?
Nay, nay, but thou to Earth wilt never take
The mission : for, obedient, humble, fair,
As ye may soar ; it is a thing, I say
That cannot be.   No spirit passes hence
To Earth.   No spirit can.   Let science shew
Thee in a moment by a trick of squares
And algebraic symbols.'

'Hold, enough'
I said, 'I know thee now, I know the why
Thou hast not reached the realm.   Poor aged soul
And scientific unit !   Take my hands.'

" It was the quick electric touch of faith,
That moved the dead old soul to life.   Old lore
Of science filled him ; but no God ; no faith.
So much of Nature's law,he knew, that law
Of other kind was deemed impossible ;
But when the circuit held him, then the spark
So fair lit up his soul ; that sweet it were
To yet recall his silent look.   He flew
Away and upward then, and now must live
Among the trustful.

      " Rising now to fall
In undulating motion on the air
I sped.   The higher scenes of beauty left
Behind, I found a less enchanting sphere ;
Yet solitary held my way.   'Tis sweet
To be alone at times.   'Tis then the plan,
Design and operation of a thought
Is compassed ; smoothed, and put in order clear.

Again 'tis good to be alone at times.
'Tis then that self, conceit disrobed, is seen
In all its naked platitude.   Then can
We question it, examine, flatter it ;
And e'en condemn unworthy action too.
And yet again 'tis ill to be alone.
For much of mischief oft comes trailing in
The orbit of our wanton star, and drags

U

It from its truer course.   But come, if hope
Can buoy a saint, may it not drown a fiend,
Or growing devil ?   Yea.   His bark is full
Of it, so full of dark and hellish hope,
At last it sinks the vessel, and he drowns
In deepest seas of machinations foul.

'Tis better then to be alone for good,
When happy thoughts and sweetest memories
Are in ascendancy.   'Tis then we cull
The fragrant blossoms of a virtue fair,
And bind a sweet bouquet to fondly place
In Honour's hand ; or weave a garland bright,
Wherewith to crown her brow.   Integrity
Is nurtured and developed fast in strength,
In grand intensity ; and forms a guard
And buttress to the tower of human form
And manly nature.

                         " To the darker belt
On to a darker world, eagerly on
I flew.   The Power that sent that which was
        borne,
Could well sustain the bearer in what form
He wished ; unto a safe alighting there
On Earth.   Barely escaping subtle verge
And far attraction of yet other suns

Than that of Earth ; anon, I saw the orb
That governs o'er a thousand million leagues,
And felt its force.   Yet kept I seeming straight
Towards it, though the knowledge of my way
Fore-present hitherto, then left me.   On
By Neptune passing soon I found my path
Was circling fast, while drawing near, its sun,
And still far distant light.   Past Uranus,
And Saturn nearing I was slowly stayed
By power occult and firm restraining.   He,
The aged seer, was right in active truth
And deed material, yet dire mistook
The motive cause and power that governed. Fast
Receding in a parabolic curve
I found my orbit winding until drawn
From out the old world sphere.   Re-traversed all
The mazy way I came until within
The realm again.   'Twas then I saw the shade
Beside me there that had arrested well
My work.   Recalled, my conscious soul declared
That moment, it was done.   A while I rest."

THE LEGEND OF THE MOSS CHAPEL.

—

It was early in the thirteenth century when Cecilia was the Lady Superior of a Convent, near Fareham, generally called the Moss, where a Knight of the name of Sir Ralph Fitz Maurice placed his beautiful daughter Elsie when he was going abroad ; out of the way of a clerk in orders named Robert de Hemisham, who they say was brother to Walter de Hemisham, of whom history speaks. This Robert had quite worried Sir Ralph in respect of his daughter. His unwelcome and intrusive attentions amounted almost to persecution. When he left his daughter here, it was for her safety and seclusion from him.

He said he would soon come again himself for her.

Sir Ralph had not been gone many days when Hemisham hearing of her whereabouts, sent two servants on horseback to demand Elsie away in the

name of her father ; who, they stated, had changed
his mind and was coming back, in fact was already
near Lewes.

The Lady Superior demurred and then refused
to give her up, unless they brought some token or
letter from Sir Ralph.

They went away, and those of the Convent heard
no more for some time.

At last one day a messenger came with a letter,
saying, that in the course of three days a party of
horsemen would arrive for Elsie ; that the leader of
the troop would show a ring as good earnest, and
that they might give her up to them. Well, this
was signed by Sir Ralph Fitz Maurice, and sure
enough on the evening of the second day, about six
or seven men-at-arms rode up. The leader of the
troop showed the Lady Superior a ring with Sir
Ralph's arms and crest engraved thereon, and
demanded Elsie ; saying that when Sir Ralph sent
before, he had hastily to go to London, wherefrom
he now sent. The ring was shown to Elsie, who
declared positively it was her father's ring, and
pressed the Lady Superior to allow her to depart,
wishing naturally enough to go to her father.
Upon this, she permitted Elsie to be escorted away
by the horsemen, who had brought a spare palfrey,
with rich trappings for her.

They journeyed by easy stages, and all went well
as far as Reigate, where they were stopped by three
other horsemen, well armed, who ordered them to
deliver up Elsie and depart ; which, much to her
surprise they did, and it was only then she began
to feel she had been entrapped. One lifted his visor
and discovered to Elsie the man her father hated
for his wild and dissolute way of life, although a
clerk in orders ; and one whom she feared and
detested herself.

They led her palfrey out of the road to a large
old mansion, so secluded as to be almost hidden
from view by the thick and varied foliage
surrounding it. A place that would be a peaceful
retreat for old age or the scholar, but the place
also that might answer for many an ill deed. It
had a broad front and high wall partly castellated
with Norman windows and arches ; a broad flight
of steps, which narrowed up almost winding to a
doorway at the side. Before they entered the
outer gate, however, one of his companions, an
honest young esquire and gentleman named Hugh
Bohun recognised Elsie, who was loudly entreating
Hemisham to take her to her father.

" Hold, Robert," cried Hugh. " This fair lady is
the daughter of a friend of my father. Is this the
lady thou talkedst of, so lightly, to us ? Is this the

demoiselle thou hast made us laugh over? Prithee, what dost thou do with this loved, unblemished child of Sir Ralph Fitz Maurice?"

"Oh, help, help me, sir, I pray thee," cried Elsie. "As thou art an honourable gentleman, take me to my father."

"Ah, thou turnest against me, Master Hugh Bohun," cried Robert.

"Nay, it is thy jest that is turned against thee," retorted Hugh.

"And thou too, traitor, coward. Draw and protect yourself."

"I give thee thy words back," returned Hugh. "*Pour Dieu et la verité*," he cried, as their swords met.

But presently Hugh became hurt in the sword arm. This for a moment confused him in his guard. Robert was about to take advantage of it in his rage, when his other companion, who also perceived it, now for the first time interfered, and peremptorily advised them to separate and go no farther.

Hugh turned to ride away, saying, "It shall not be for long. I will be with thee again shortly."

Robert laughed in reply, thinking of his triumph and turned to Elsie, who now was weeping. "Why

doth thou weep fair one?" said he. "Thou
mayst choose thine own time to give me thine
hand. I have but taken the precaution to have
thee nearer to me that I may better woo thee.
Attendants await to conduct thee to thine apartments."

"Where is my father?" she asked. "How
camest thou with his ring?"

"Oh, fair lady, that was but a drollery," he
answered, "one that was made like his. I well
remember the ring he wore."

"And the letter?"

"A counterfeit," he answered with a bow.
"Seest thou what love will accomplish at
times."

"Call ye it love to deceive and decoy a girl
from the house in which her father left her for
safety? Wretch, know that I will die ere I look
on thee otherwise than as a dog."

Here his face changed to that of a fiend, and he
would have threatened her. Still, thinking to gain
his end afterwards, he only smiled as she walked
to her apartments majestically.

Robert, then, after giving whispered orders to
his menials, rode away with his other companion,
intending to remove her again the next day to mislead
Hugh.

Now early in the morning of this same day, as the story hath it, Sir Ralph Fitz Maurice himself rode up to the Convent of the Moss and asked for his daughter. You may imagine the consternation the sisters felt at this demand. At last they told how they had been deceived, and all about the letter and ring.

" Did I not say, I would come myself? " cried he. He stamped and swore, and showed them his ring, saying it was all a foul lie. At last he galloped off, vowing that if he did not find her that day, he would come back, and raze the walls to the ground, an awful sacrilege at that time.

He sometimes thought it was a trick to hide his daughter for the cloisters; though mostly his thoughts went back to Hemisham. Knowing he had a house near Dorking or Reigate, he actually traced them on the road near to those places; when he suddenly lost all clue of them, and turned into Dorking to rest at his friend William de Gretham's house.

We must turn back again now to Hugh Bohun, who went away wounded. He, after having his wound properly dressed by a leech hard by, immediately sought the leader of the small troop of men who brought Elsie to the place, and who knew nothing yet of his quarrel with Hemisham.

"Well," said he to the man. "Foundest it an easy matter to do, didst thou not?"

"Yes, truly, but I feel well rid of the charge, and I could wish the pretty lady a better husband."

Hugh laughed seemingly to think it was a good joke.

"Heyday," continued the man. "It is no affair of mine, and little I know of it, beyond who she is. If it is true what I hear, it will go hard yet with Master Hemisham."

"How, what's that?" asked Hugh.

"Well, I am told by one who knows Sir Ralph, that he was seen hard riding on the road to Dorking," said he, thinking that Hugh knew all along who it was he had been sent for.

"To Dorking!" exclaimed Hugh, who whistled to himself, knowing it was his friend Master Gretham, Hugh's cousin, whom he would go to.

"Yes, it was Sir Ralph or his ghost," said the fellow.

"Holy Mary, preserve us!" exclaimed Hugh crossing himself. "I thought he was drowned."

"And so does Master Hemisham, I believe," answered the man. "I must seek him so I may warn him Sir Ralph is close by."

"I will do that; take no further heed of it." said Hugh.

" What's that, why wounded, sir?" said the fellow, noticing the dressing of Hugh's arm.

Hugh had previously been careful to hide this, but his impulse at the information caused him to discover it, by forgetting for the moment to keep his arm in one position.

" Only a dog's bite," answered Hugh, " of little consequence ; I dare say I shall be even with the brute yet. In the meantime here is something to toast thy fellows with." He threw him some gold, adding presently, " Thou needst not say thou hast seen me ; I would have the conceit of this information myself. Good even."

" Good even, and welcome, sir," said the man. " Now for a merry carouse, my mates ; now for a merry carouse."

Then Hugh galloped off, presently turning into the road to Dorking.

Now Hemisham, having conceived an idea that he ought to get Elsie out of the way sooner, to avoid whatever Hugh Bohun intended, and maybe he had heard the rumour later about Sir Ralph, thought to remove her that same night instead of the following day. He went to the house for that purpose, calling up an old woman to go and tell Elsie she must ride forth at once. Elsie had retired to rest, however, and was slumbering soundly after the trials and fatigues of the day ; doubtless dreaming through her tears of her father and of the one who had tried to protect her.

" What is that ? Who is there ? " she exclaimed in a waking fright at the loud knocking at the room door.

" It is I—Janet," cried the old woman. " Master Robert declares ye must ride forth from here this very hour. Will you be rising ? "

" Oh ! I cannot go away to-night with him," she cried.

" Defy him not. He must go and thou with him," quoth a man's voice, in which she recognised that of Hemisham. " Be at the gate in a quarter-of-an hour or he will fetch thee. Thy palfrey is waiting."

" Oh, Heaven protect me ! " she cried, weeping.

Elsie hastily dressed, taking care that her poniard was ready at hand. Yet she did not intend to go down the staircase.

Then she knelt down to pray for protection, and while so doing, Bang ! bang ! sounded on the door, now burst open by Hemisham ; who lifted her up, and carried her down the stairs : weeping all the way and screaming for help. No one appeared. Should she use her poniard ? Could she use it ?

Could she muster courage to stab herself or wound her persecutor? These were the questions she was hurriedly asking herself.

By this time, at the foot of the steps leading to the gravel pathway, the impulse came, in addition to its being easier from her position, to wound him rather than herself, and she quickly drew the dagger and thrust it in his side.

A poor thrust at best, yet it caused him to fall, throwing her heavily from him. He cursed and moaned : but presently seemed to recover himself a little. He had risen, when there came dashing up two horsemen.

" My child, Elsie, my child," cried Sir Ralph Fitz Maurice, for it was he and Hugh Bohun.

Elsie had swooned away and heard nothing.

" Dastard ! Villain ! " cried Sir Ralph to Hemisham. " Draw for your life. What dost thou with my child ? Draw."

Now by this time Hemisham was weak and there was not sufficient light for Sir Ralph to see he was wounded ; which had he seen, might have qualified Sir Ralph's onset ; for even not wounded, Hemisham was never a match for a warrior like Sir Ralph.

So it came about that Hemisham was soon disabled and received a mortal blow. As he fell he said :

"Elsie is not hurt. She is only affrighted."

"Come Elsie," said her father to her as she came to her senses, "come, it is thy father ; come away from this wolf's den. What ho," called he aloud to the servants who now appeared at hearing so much noise. "Ho there, bring lights, attend, ye miscreants, to thy master—a base dastard who has tried to steal my child. He hath his reward now, and one that is fit for such as he. Come Hugh, come Elsie, away. Hugh I have to thank thee for our being in time to save her."

And they rode away back to Dorking, Elsie being a long time under the impression that she had killed Hemisham herself. It was only after a second swoon, at the house at Dorking, that it was explained and she was reassured.

Now Sir Ralph having found his daughter that day, felt a kind of compunction for having thought so sacrilegiously about the Moss ; and after some days returned thither with his daughter and Bohun, who now was established in high favour with both the father and daughter. It was by way of penance he made this journey ; although not at all convinced that the sisters were not guilty of a great breach of trust.

As they neared the convent they saw to their astonishment that it was in flames. Upon approaching it they found no one was injured, yet, the sisters, one and all, told them, that they had severally dreamed of, or seen a figure, on the same night as the attempt to carry Elsie away was frustrated by her father, warning them all to prepare for the destruction of their building, which should be seen by Elsie and her father.

Sir Ralph wished to build a new chapel, but as Cecilia shortly and unaccountably died of no particular disease that they could discover or understand in those days, the church authorities thought the place would never prosper ; so Sir Ralph built one elsewhere, where, the story says, Hugh and Elsie were afterwards united.

THE END.

www.ingramcontent.com/pod-product-compliance
Lightning Source LLC
Chambersburg PA
CBHW031403270326
41929CB00010BA/1308